SPIR...

LEADERSHIP

Orman Press Inc.

Spiritual Leadership

A Guide to Developing Spiritual Leaders in the Church

Published by

Orman Press, Inc.
4200 Sandy Lake Drive
Lithonia, GA 30038
T. 770.808.0999
F. 770.808.1955
E-mail. Ormanmcc@aol.com
http://www.Ormanpress.com

Preface

This book is the product of 15 years of work. During that time I have studied, read, and conducted leadership training workshops with church leaders from all over the country. My interest in the subject goes back to my initial days at Second Calvary Baptist Church in Norfolk, Virginia. It became clear to me that if we were going to be successful, we would need trained leaders. I was interested in developing a climate wherein leaders could be trained and equipped to lead small groups in the church.

During my doctor of Ministry studies at Howard University in Washington, D.C., I tried to answer this question: What is the most effective means to develop small group leaders in the church? My studies helped spur my interest in learning more about leadership.

I want to thank the members of Second Calvary for serving as a laboratory for many of my ideas and thoughts on leadership. Our congregation has benefited from my personal quest to learn more about the factors that produce effective leaders. There are numerous people and churches from all over the country who have listened to me and invited me to lead workshops. Thank you for the opportunities you have given to me.

I am especially grateful to my wife, Rosetta, who has been a constant source of encouragement and strength. I am grateful to her for reading the manuscript and offering comments. I am thankful to Stephanie Jackson, who read the manuscript and offered suggestions and encouragement. Thank you very much!

The question is obviously going to be raised: Why do we need another book on leadership? My answer is simple: we have not exhausted the subject. As long as there are people on the face of the earth, there will be a need to understand leadership. Besides, there is a need for leadership from an African American perspective. I have borrowed thoughts and suggestions from many people. I trust that this presentation will be a blessing to all who read it.

In the Introduction I consider the nature of leadership and its definition. In Chapter One I discuss the context of our leadership, which is the church. It is important that spiritual leaders have a fully developed biblical and theological understanding of the church. The focus is on understanding what the New Testament teaches about the church. In Chapter Two I develop a theology of leadership, which is the framework for church leadership. In this chapter we try to understand what the New Testament teaches about leadership by looking at Jesus. Chapter Three focuses on spiritual leadership. The chapter is an attempt to develop a portrait of what spiritual leaders look like.

In Chapter Four the duties of spiritual leaders are discussed. What are the duties of spiritual leaders? What are their responsibilities to the church? Chapter Four is an attempt to answer that question. Chapter Five is where we examine the ministry of the pastor. One of the most important issues addressed is the spiritual authority of the pastor. Chapter Six is a discussion of the roles of key leaders in the church. In Chapter Seven the unique challenges that face Black Church leaders are discussed. In Chapter Eight there is discussion of the issues that relate to leading change in the church.

Chapter Nine focuses on the importance of having both vision and courage, in order to bring about change. Chapter Ten is my treatment of the subject of motivation and its role in developing strong congregational leaders. Chapter Eleven concludes the book with a discussion of leadership training.

Special thanks to all of my friends in ministry who have helped to inspire this work. God bless each of you!

Geoffrey V. Guns

"Dr. Geoffrey V. Guns has provided for the reader the distillations of more than 20 years of study, of insights gained from successfully pastoring a congregation, and of the lessons learned from the give and take involved in leading associations. He has not only given of himself but he has labored to harness and activate the energies of all the people and to develop the potential of God's people to effectively do the work of God. He writes with clarity and conviction. His points are biblically based and practically proven. They provide foci around which spiritual lay leadership can be recruited and nourished. We are indebted to Dr. Guns for his mind to share and for the product of his labors. I recommend this book be added to your library of Helps in Christian Ministry."

Dr. William J. Shaw, President
National Baptist Convention, U.S.A., Inc.

Contents

Introduction

During the past fifty years, considerable attention has been given to the subject of leadership by the business community, non-profit organizations, para-church groups, churches, religious denominations, academic institutions and the social sciences. Leadership is probably one of the most talked about and used organizational words today. Everyone is looking for people who are effective leaders.

Many studies and experiments have been conducted to determine what constitutes effective leadership and what are the factors that give rise to it. Indeed, as Bernard Bass has written, "Leadership is one of the world's oldest preoccupations. The understanding of leadership has figured strongly in the quest for knowledge."[1]

Leaders have existed since the beginning of creation. The Old and New Testaments are filled with the stories of the lives of men and women who were tribal and national leaders. The writings of ancient civilizations are filled with the exploits of heroes who have come to us in history as great leaders. Bass stated that "myths and legends about great leaders were important in the development of civilized societies."[2] Names such as Alexander the Great, the Pharaoh of Egypt, Moses, and King David all create within our minds images of great leaders. These are men who achieved greatness because of their exploits. Even in the modern era, Absalom Jones, Adam Clayton Powell, and Martin Luther King, Jr. are all men who are remembered as great leaders. Gary Yukl has stated that much of the history of human civilization is the story of the lives of military, political, religious and social leaders.[3] He went on to say, "The exploits of brave and clever leaders are the essence of many legends and myths."[4]

Yet the question remains as to what made them great leaders. More importantly is the question of what made them effective leaders. How do we measure the effectiveness of a leader in a given situation and context? Are there any traits that are uniquely associated with leadership effectiveness? Can one be taught to be an effective leader? Is effectiveness in leadership a combination of traits, both natural and learned? Are there lessons we can learn from the ancient biblical leaders that will help us today? Can spirituality be taught? In this book I hope to answer some of these questions. For some of them, I will only scratch the surface.

Leadership Defined

What is leadership? This is a question we need to try and answer early on in our study. It goes without saying that there are numerous definitions of leadership. In his classic work on leadership, Ralph Stogdill stated that there are as many defini-tions of leadership as there are people defining it.[5] It all depends on who you are talking to and the context of that discussion. You could be talking about leadership in the military, which is quite different from leadership in the corporate world, which is quite different from leadership in the civic community, which is quite different from leadership in political organizations, which is quite different from leadership in the church of Jesus Christ. This book is about leadership within the context of the African American Christian church. And more specifically, it is intended to assist small group leaders or ministry (formerly called auxiliary) leaders. It is the context of the church which shapes and determines our understanding of leadership. You cannot effectively lead in the church unless you understand its spiritual nature, purpose, organization, and various functions. Lack of spiritual insight and understanding is a major reason church leaders fail.

Leadership has been defined in many ways. Let me give my definition of leadership. Leadership is the process of getting a group of people to willingly work together toward a common goal or objective. There are several key factors that relate to this definition.

First, leadership is a process. The word process has in it thoughts of a step-by-step method. It denotes order and direction. Many young, inexperienced clergy and lay leaders fail because they do not recognize that leadership is more than just being elected. It is a matter of learning how to get things done in an orderly manner through a group of people. In voluntary organizations, such as churches and para-church organizations, coercion, intimidation and demanding does not work. Volunteers will quit when they are forced to served. Leaders must be able to motivate their followers to serve.

Second, leadership involves a group of people. You cannot stake any claims to being a leader, without followers. There must be at least two other people in order to comprise a group. Sometimes leaders are called to lead people who are from various backgrounds and who have no relationship to anyone in the group. Within the context of the church, leaders are often called to lead large and small groups of people to achieve various goals during the course of a year. Leaders within the church must master the art of leading groups and working with people.

Third, leadership is the process of getting people to willingly work together. It is essential that leaders understand the art of getting people to work together. Nehemiah is a very good example of a leader who was able to galvanize various groups of people into a cohesive team (see Nehemiah 3). He was able to get his people to work together to rebuild the wall around Jerusalem in fifty-two days (Nehemiah 6:15). There may be times when a group goes through a series of cycles before they are galvanized into a cohesive working group. The leader must know how to lead the group through decision-making, conflict, problem-solving, discussions and other activities that can potentially destroy a group's effectiveness and togetherness. These activities do not necessarily have to be destructive. Skillful leaders are able to help groups make decisions in a way that is not disruptive to the group. Sometimes the group's goals can be sabotaged by the very people who are assigned to work toward achieving it. Leaders must develop skills at getting things done. There are many other definitions that could have been used, but this one fits our context more precisely. The most important thing that a leader does is lead. Without the leader leading, the group stands a good chance of failing. In the coming chapters, we will take a look at group leadership in greater detail. The church has a real need for leaders who are spiritual and effective.

Leadership Effectiveness

How do you measure the effectiveness of a leader? As Yukl has pointed out, measuring leadership effectiveness is as varied as the writer who does it.[6] Leaders need to be able to determine if they are having an impact upon the organization. Unless we have criteria to measure our effectiveness, we may be failing while believing we are succeeding. Yukl has identified three criteria that have been used for evaluating the effectiveness of a leader.[7]

- Organizational effectiveness
- Follower satisfaction
- Leader contribution to group process

Let's take a look at these three criteria. Organizational effectiveness refers to the extent to which the group is able to meet its goals and carry out its mission. A pastor's leadership effectiveness may be measured by such things as whether or not attendance increases, annual giving increases, new programs and ministries begun, the level of participation in church programs and activities, and the overall spiritual growth of the congregation or individual members. The growth of the church or a church group is a clear sign of leadership effectiveness.

Follower satisfaction refers to how they feel about their leader. Do the members of the group respect the leader? Is he or she trustworthy? Are they willing to follow the leader? Do the members feel that the leader possesses ministry competence? How members feel about the leader is important for organizational effectiveness.

Sometimes leaders can wreck their own efforts by displaying the negative attitudes that are picked up by group members. Leaders can engender hostility toward themselves by the way they interact with group members. Sometimes leaders can loose the confidence of group members by simply ignoring their concerns. All of these can kill the effectiveness of the leader and thwart group efforts.

Group process refers to how the leader handles the group. Does he or she understand the dynamics of group behavior? How does the leader handle difficult people and difficult situations? Does the leader erupt into vocal attacks when group members disagree with the leader? Does the leader understand how to move a group through the various stages of conflict? Does the leader contribute to group unity? Does the leader help the group to achieve its goals? If you learn to help those whom you lead reach their personal goals, they will help you achieve the group's goals.

Many leaders in the church fail because they do not understand how groups work and how to lead a group of people. Later in the book we will look at specific areas of group leadership that are vital to ministry success.

Are Leaders Necessary?

One of the questions that this book seeks to answer is the question of the necessity of leaders. Leaders are vital to the survival and effectiveness of any organization. Effective leaders will invariably lead their organizations to achieve their goals. Leaders do make the difference. Bass has noted that leaders make the difference between their organization's success or failure.[8] Organizations without effective leadership will always have a difficult time succeeding. Without leaders, organizations will flounder and never reach their goals. It is said that Napoleon once stated he would rather see an army of rabbits led by a lion than see an army of lions led by a rabbit.[9] A leader with a rabbit mentality will lead like a rabbit, fearful and unsure about the future. The lion is the king of the jungle, and his very stature demands respect from all of the other animals in the jungle.

In many African American churches, we start with how much something is going to cost us. We never begin with what are the benefits of us doing this or that, rather how many dollars does this cost? We bring this same kind of thinking to calling pastors. Many African American churches have not realized the importance of recruiting the best available pastoral candidates, nor have we recognized the absolute necessity of developing lay leaders. I have often talked to pulpit committees who are looking to find a new pastor who fits their budget. Their quest for a new pastoral leader is not driven by the needs of the congregation, but rather by what they are willing to pay a pastor. The Chicago Bulls, prior to drafting Michael Jordan, were a middle of the pact franchise. No one ever really expected Chicago to compete or contend for the NBA championship. But one man made the difference in the thinking and performance of the other players. It goes without saying that had Chicago's ownership been driven by budget constraints and not getting the best player available, the result would have been different.

Leaders are the key to organizational success. An effective leader can take a struggling organization and turn it completely around. Effective leaders inspire and instill confidence in the people and lead them to do great things. Leaders are central to organizational performance. Leaders inspire their people to go beyond themselves. Leaders encourage their people by letting them know that when things are difficult, they can have hope. Leaders inspire their people to believe in themselves and that no obstacle or task is too great for them. Leaders get things done!

The opposite side of the coin is a leader who is ineffective, who generates despondency in his/her followers and fails at everything. Ineffective leaders are identified by their record of failures, missed opportunities, despair among the followers and a lack of measurable results. God does not call us to failure, but success!

Leadership Nugget: **Leadership is not something mystical and ethereal that cannot be understood by ordinary people. It is a myth that only a lucky few can ever decipher the leadership code.** (Kouzes and Posner, *The Leadership Challenge*)

Leadership in the Church

In recent years, the Christian church has begun to take the need for effective leaders seriously. Many churches are beginning to conduct leadership programs to train lay persons for Christian leadership responsibilities. There is a real need for more African American churches to develop programs to train lay leaders.

Unfortunately, many seminaries and Bible colleges have not gotten the message that preachers need to be trained in leadership, as well as homiletics, hermeneutics, history and theology. One of the things that baffles me is the inability of seminaries to recognize that leading the African American church today, and in the twenty-first century, will require a different set of leadership skills. African Americans are more affluent, better educated, better exposed and hold positions of management in major corporations. Therefore, the pastoral and lay leaders of the future will need to be better equipped to serve. The church of the twenty-first century will need leaders who are going to be effective in leading God's people in the future.

There are a number of studies conducted and books written on the subject of leadership. Many of these studies use the corporate motivation for increased profits as the starting point for understanding effective leadership. There is nothing wrong with these studies. I have used them myself and have relied heavily upon those who have done extensive work in the study of leadership. The African American church should examine the research and work that has been used to develop better leaders in the corporate world. There is something that can be learned from the secular community when it comes to leadership development.

There is one thing that we need to keep in mind and, that is, the difference between the church and secular organizations. Unlike other sectors of society, the starting point for the church is its theological and biblical understanding of the nature of the church and its mission in the world. We are the people of God, called to carry out the purpose of God. And we know that all things work together for good to those who love God, to those who are called according to His purpose (Romans 8:28 NKJV).

The pastor of the local church cannot be compared to the CEO of a major corporation. The pastor is not judged nor evaluated on whether or not market share has increased, business is growing, profitability is up and the company's share price is rising. The pastor is God's man or woman who has been called to lead God's people. The office of pastor/teacher is unique. He is the undershepherd to the flock of God. Later in the book, we will take a more detailed look at the office of pastor. The pastor needs the help and assistance of other leaders in the church in order to be effective in his office. A classic example of this can be seen in Moses. Moses wanted to do everything by himself. He was encouraged by Jethro, his father in law, to enlist the help of other leaders (see Exodus 18:13).

This book is written with the African American church in mind. It can be used by anyone who seeks a deeper understanding of spiritual leadership and its importance to the church. One of the things that I have observed over the years is our inability to recognize that we are only as strong as the leaders who lead in our churches. This is not to say that there are not spiritual, strong, able, knowledgeable, effective leaders in our churches. Rather, I am saying that in many of our churches, our leaders have not been trained on how to be a spiritual leader in the church.

There are several reasons why leadership training is not widely used as a means for increasing organizational effectiveness in many African American churches. **First**, leadership is not a subject that many preachers get excited about. We are more prone to want to develop our preaching and teaching skills. **Second**, very few pastors see leadership training as the cure for many of the ills of their churches. Poorly organized programs and lack of motivation by followers have their genesis in poorly trained leaders. Leadership training includes learning how to be a good follower as well as leader. **Third**, there are many ineffective pastors who have never had a course or read a book on the subject of leadership. They have learned to lead by following the examples of their pastors. Some of the models we pattern ourselves after may not be very good models. **Fourth**, many pastors still want to do, run, and control everything. Some leaders are threatened by the presence of a person of equal or greater strength.

The African American or Black church is the context for our leadership. (We will talk more about the context of our leadership in the next chapter.) We lead a people who have come out of a background of oppression and racism. We lead people who have been victimized by the politics of a disinterested political structure. We lead a people who grew up sitting on the back of the bus. Leadership in the African American church means helping a younger generation remember the struggles and road over which we have come. Leadership in the Black church is different than leadership in the White church. Blacks and

Whites think and act differently about church and in church. George Gallup, Jr. and D. Michael Lindsay published a major study in 1999 that surveyed the religious beliefs and trends in America. Their study confirms the fact that Blacks and Whites think differently about religion and the church.

A higher proportion of Blacks take their religion seriously and practice it more ardently in comparison to people of other races. Blacks in this country are far more likely than Whites to consider religion "very important" in their own lives (82% compared to 58%). Blacks are more likely than Whites to think religion not only is very important but also can answer all or most of today's problems (86% to 62%). Few Blacks or Whites, however, see the impact of religion increasing in this country (27% each). Participation in the affairs of the local church usually is higher among Blacks than Whites. Over eight Blacks in ten (82%) say they are church members, 50% report they attend church at least once during the previous week, and 43% claim church attendance is a weekly practice. Statistically, just about every Black adult believes in God or a universal spirit. Seven in ten (70%) believe in the devil, and even more think there is a hell (74%). Nearly all Blacks (97%) believe there is a heaven.

In the African American community, the church is at the center of community life. Many things begin in the church. The church is where we meet. It is the social and political epicenter of our community. Therefore, it is only natural that we would attempt to understand leadership in that context. The central thesis of this book is that the key to ministry effectiveness lies with training lay leaders how to lead effectively. It is the work of the pastor to equip the saints for the work of the ministry (see Ephesians 4:11-16). A part of the work of equipping the saints is training leaders to lead.

Christian Leadership Defined

Christian leadership is accepting the call of God to use your spiritual gifts and talents to advance the work of the kingdom of God among and with a specific group of people. This definition makes several points about the distinctiveness of Christian leadership. **First**, Christian leadership is first and foremost a call from God. God calls men and women for His purposes (see Exodus 3:1; Jeremiah 1:1-9; Amos 7:15-16; Galatians 1:15-16). **Second**, Christian leadership involves using our spiritual gifts for kingdom work and service. God gives us gifts of grace to use in the exercise of our Christian leadership (see Romans 12:3-6; 1 Corinthians 12:7-11). **Third**, Christian leadership takes place within the context of the Christian church, which makes it different from leadership in any other context. The church is the community of the faithful who have repented of their sins, been baptized and filled with the Holy Spirit, and have answered God's call to mission and ministry.

The Context of Our Leadership

"And I also say to you that you are Peter, and upon this rock, I will build my church; and the gates of Hades shall not prevail over it."

Matthew 16:18

Prior to discussing Christian leadership in greater detail, we must examine the context of our leadership, i.e., the church. It is important that our understanding of who we are called to be and what we are called to do be drawn from the Scriptures. This discussion about the church is not going to be detailed.[1] Any such attempt in such a limited space would be futile and presumptuous. Rather, this is merely an attempt to establish the spiritual and local context for Christian leadership, which is the church.

In recent years we have seen a move by churches and denominations to recapture the evangelistic zeal of the early Christian church, particularly the militant picture that is set forth in the Scriptures. During the latter years of the twentieth century, the church of Jesus Christ lost much of its spiritual presence and power. God has begun a radical revitalization of the church that is being manifested in many ways. Churches have begun to reorganize themselves around the purpose of evangelism and ministry. Many churches are adopting a small groups model as a means of enhancing member participation in ministry and missions. Throughout the ages, the church has remained God's answer to human isolation and alienation. Through the church, God is addressing the human conditions of brokenness and alienation. The church is still the instrument of God for human reconciliation and redemption. In the next few pages we will examine the biblical teachings regarding the church.

The Origin of the Church

Let's begin by considering the origin of the church. When did the church begin and who started it? The church is not of human origin. Nor is the church the product of human creativity. Humanity could not invent anything that even approximates the church. The church's origin is deeply woven within the divine intention and will of God (see 1 Timothy 3:5, 15). God the Father, had ordained the existence of the church before the foundation of the world had been laid. He chose us in Him before the foundation of the world, that we should be holy and without blame before Him in love, having predestined us to adoption as sons by Jesus Christ to Himself, according to the good pleasure of His will (Ephesians 1:4-5 NKJV). The church is a manifestation in time of an eternal purpose that was hidden in God.[2]

The Christian Church was historically founded by Jesus Christ. Jesus responded to Peter's statement identifying Him as the "Son of the Living God" by saying, "And I also say to you that you are Peter, and on this rock I will build My church, and the gates of Hades shall not prevail against it" (Matthew 16:18). Joe Ellis stated that "the church is both the product of God's purpose and the means for achieving it."[3]

Throughout the first century, Satan raised up opposition against the church and tried to stamp it out (see Acts 4:1-23; 5:17-39; 6:8-15, 51-60; 11:19). Satan used people who were caught up in their own religious traditions as instruments of rage against the church. It was God's church that Paul admitted to persecuting (see Acts 8:3; 1 Corinthians 15:9). Paul tried to stop the spread and growth of the church.

The church draws its life from the Holy Spirit, who gives it life and power (see Acts 2:4). It was on the day of Pentecost when the Holy Spirit came and gave birth to the church of Jesus Christ. Everyone who was present in the house was filled with the Holy Spirit. On that day the first Christian sermon was preached by the Apostle Peter (see Acts 2:14). G. Willis Bennett noted that "one dominant factor which makes the Church different from other social groups is its identification with Jesus Christ."[4] It has been sent by Jesus to preach the gospel and make disciples of all men and women (see Matthew 28:18-20). The church is that community of people who find in Jesus Christ the clue to the meaning of life and God's purposes for His creation. The church is God's people seeking to achieve His purpose in the world (see Romans 8:28).

Old Testament Origins

The church has its roots in the Old Testament with the call of Abraham to become the patriarch of a new nation. "Now the

Lord said to Abram: 'Get out of your country, from your family and from your father's house, to a land that I will show you. And I will make you a great nation; I will bless you and make your name great and you shall be a blessing. I will bless those who bless you, and I will curse him who curses you; and in you all the families of the earth shall be blessed'" (Genesis 12:1-2 NKJV).

The deliverance from bondage in Egypt was the beginning of the new nation of Israel. Israel was called into a special covenant relationship with God through Abraham (see Exodus 19:5-6; Deuteronomy 7:6-8). Lindgren and Shawchuck noted that "God's call to Abraham and the covenant initiated with Israel at that time continues through Christ and the New Israel of the New Testament community."[5]

Bennett remarked that "God's covenant relationship with Israel designated the people as special, as is seen in the Hebrew phrase **Yahweh gahal**, usually translated 'assembly of the Lord' or congregation of the Lord."[6]   In the Old Testament the Hebrew word **qahal** expresses the idea of an assembly of God.[7]   In Deuteronomy, **qahal** means above all the congregation gathered to conclude the covenant at Sinai (Deuteronomy 9:10; 10:4).[8] The congregation of the Lord came to signify the people who were bound to keep God's commandments by virtue of the covenant (see Joshua 1:5-9).   God's deliverance from slavery in Egypt began the covenant relationship between God and Israel.   It was the ratification of the covenant on Mt. Sinai that established Israel as God's chosen possession (see Exodus 19:1-6).   They were to be a kingdom of priests. As God's people, Israel was commanded to consecrate themselves to the Lord (see Exodus 19:10).

The New Testament Ekklesia

The English word church comes from the Greek word **ekklesia**, and means those who have been called out. Peter wrote that the church is made up of those whom God has called out of darkness: "But you are a CHOSEN RACE, A ROYAL PRIESTHOOD, A HOLY NATION, A PEOPLE for God's own possession, that you may proclaim the excellencies of Him who has called you out of darkness into His marvelous light" (1 Peter 2:9 NASB). The church is made up of those who were, at one time, lost and alien to God's promises (see Ephesians 2:11, 19). These are the ones whom God has redeemed through the shed blood of Jesus Christ (see Ephesians 1:7; Hebrews 9:12-14). In the church, we find those who have been recreated by God and made new creatures in Christ (see 2 Corinthians 5:17; Ephesians 2:10).

Through the church, the gospel is preached and men and women are brought into a new relationship with God (Romans 5:1-10). When Peter preached the first Christian sermon under the anointing of the Holy Spirit, three thousand souls were saved (Acts 2:40-41). There was such a demonstration of the power of the Holy Spirit that people were saved daily (Acts 2:47). Even members of the priesthood confessed faith in the resurrection of Jesus Christ (Acts 6:7). Through the ministry of the first Christians, people were healed and restored to health (Acts 5:16; 8:5-8). Intense persecution of the church caused the saints to move beyond Jerusalem. As they went, they carried the gospel and new congregations began to spring up (Acts 11:19). The church is the end time people of God who are called to be His ambassadors of light and life (see Acts 2:14-16).

New Testament Church Metaphors

The New Testament uses many metaphors to describe the people of God and who we are as the Church. I am going to list a few of them for you. The Church is called the body of Christ (1 Corinthians 12:27); the branches (John 15:1); the household of faith (Galatians 6:10); the flock of God (Acts 20:28); the bride of Christ (Ephesians 5:20-31); the chosen ones (Luke 18:7); Abraham's seed (Galatians 3:29); church of the firstborn (Hebrews 12:23); the congregation of the saints (1 Corinthians 14:33); the dwelling of God (Ephesians 2:22); God's field and God's building (1 Corinthians 3:9); the family of God (1 Peter 4:17); the people of God (Matthew 1:22); the sons of God (Romans 8:14).

The church is not a physical building, it is a spiritual building that has been fitly joined together by Jesus Christ. "In whom the whole building, being fitted together, grows into a whole temple in the Lord, in whom you are also being built together for a dwelling place of God in the Spirit" (Ephesians 2:21-22; see also 4:16). The church is not a political action committee, nor is it a purely social change agent. The church engages in political action when the rights of the poor are disregarded by the political institutions. The church engages in social action because Jesus called us to be socially responsible (see Matthew 25:31-46). The church is not a denomination. Although denominations exist today, Jesus never set out to found nor form a denomination. Denominations are not all bad; they have their place. They are the results of the inability of Christians to agree totally on the content of our faith and how the Bible is interpreted.

One of the lessons we want to gain from this study is that the church is a spiritual organism. It is not a static, one way only organization. Indeed, the church must be thought of as a living organism which gains its life from God. As an organism, the church has the capacity to grow and transform itself into what God wants it to be.

The Church As a Fellowship

Bennett has ably pointed out that "at least two words from the New Testament must be understood to capture the essence of the Church: ekklesia and koinonia."[9] The word koinonia is generally translated as fellowship and has the meaning of sharing, partnership or participation (see Acts 4:32; Philippians 1:5; 3:15). The early Church found new life and power in the concept of sharing one with another in worship, witnessing, breaking bread together and even in the corporate use of possessions (Acts 2:42).[10] Luke recorded their gatherings: "And they were continually devoting themselves to the apostle's teaching and to fellowship, to the breaking of bread and to prayer" (Acts 2:42 NASB). There emerged within the church at Jerusalem, a connectedness that had not been seen before. There was genuine love and concern evidenced. The church members shared their belongings and cared for each other. They held things in a common pool to be shared by all (see Acts 4:32). Joe Ellis remarked, "In this remarkable relationship, Christians shared each other's hurts, weaknesses, personal problems, material needs, aspirations, prayer concerns and victories."[11] They developed relationships that were akin to those of a family. Jesus called those who did the will of the Father, his brothers and sisters (see Mark 3:35).

This new community of believers in Jesus Christ were bound together by the presence and power of the Holy Spirit, which was operative among them beginning on Pentecost (see Acts 2:1). It was the Holy Spirit who empowered them for preaching and teaching (see Acts 4:31). They were people who moved and lived under the inspiration of the Holy Spirit. They even selected leaders who were men that had demonstrated a high level of spirituality (see Acts 6:3).

For the Apostle Paul, fellowship was not just a human relationship, rather, it was a spiritual relationship between the believer and Jesus Christ. God calls believers into fellowship with Jesus Christ, who is both the Son of God and our Lord (see 1 Corinthians 1:9). The believer lives in the flesh; yet it is the fellowship of the Spirit that continues to unite believers to Christ and one another (see Philippians 2:1). We can share in the sufferings of Christ because of our fellowship with Him (see Philippians 3:10). Because of our fellowship with Jesus, we are to have no fellowship with darkness and sin (see 2 Corinthians 6:14). "Similarly, *Koinonia* in 1 Cor. 10:16 means 'participation' in the body and blood of Christ and thus union with the exalted Christ. This fellowship with Christ comes about through the transformation of man to the very roots of his being."[12]

The challenge before the contemporary church is to reclaim that sense of fellowship and connectedness that is ours by spiritual birthright. We must reclaim the promise of God and the renewal of the spirit of power and boldness that lies dormant within us. If the African American church is going to be the agent of spiritual, social, political and communal transformation, then we must recapture the essence of the biblical model of the church. Fellowship forms the foundation from which we can begin to strengthen groups and leaders to become more evangelical and ministry focused. The church cannot be built on a biblical model of fellowship and love, while members live in social isolation from one another. There is a real need for churches to discover new ways of bringing about social inter-action and connection in a world that prizes privacy. Jesus commanded His disciples to display the quality of love that would unmistakably identify them with Him. "A new commandment I give to you, that you love one another, even as I have loved you, that you also love one another. By this all men will know that you are My disciples, if you have love for one another" (John 13:34-35 NASB). The church cannot be the biblical image of Christ and not be in partnership with its community. We are most like Jesus when we live out the incarnation (see Matthew 4:23-25; John 1:14) and carry out the mandate to do ministry in the world (see Matthew 25:31-46).

God calls us to share the gospel of salvation with those in our communities, just as the Samaritan woman Jesus met at the well did. She ran back to town and told everyone about the man she had met who told her all that she had ever done (see John 4:28-30, 39-41). As we share the gospel of God's redemptive love, we become one with those in the communities of our churches.

There are too many churches who have no community connection. They neither do ministry in nor with the community where they are located. In many instances, these congregations and their places of worship go virtually unnoticed by the community. When the church fails to reach out to its community, it may be perceived as being isolationist in its thinking.[13] As a spiritual community of faith, the church of Jesus Christ must never be afflicted with a condition of introversion. The larger community is the church's field of labor. We are called to first go to those who live within the immediate surroundings of the church.

The ministry of the apostles began in Jerusalem, spread to Judea and Samaria, and then to the ends of the earth (Acts 1:8; 8:1; 11:1). Community and fellowship cannot be created without the creation of spiritual relationships within the body (see Romans 12:9-21; Ephesians 4:22-32). Healthy relationships are the foundation for building community in the local church. As we create biblical communities, we begin to live out the mandate of Christ--to preach the gospel to the ends of the earth and make disciples of those who are lost (see Matthew 28:18-20).

The Purpose of the Church

The original mandate given by Jesus to His first disciples has not changed with the passage of time.

And Jesus came and spoke to them saying, "All authority has been given to Me in heaven and earth. Go therefore and make disciples of all nations, baptizing them in the name of the Father and of the Son and of the Holy Spirit." (Matthew 28:18-20)

Our mission was and remains, "Go ye into all the world and preach, teach, and evangelize the lost." The church exists for a distinct purpose, and even though the social context in which the church exists is constantly evolving, the mission remains unchanged.

The church must develop ministries that will be relevant for the twenty-first century. By relevant, I mean that the ministry of the church will have meaning for those it seeks to reach. We have a message for the hopeless and the hurting. As we live out the ethic of love in our midst, others will be attracted by our unique relationship to God and one another.

How does the African American church fulfill its purpose in the world? The church must be actively involved in every facet of life, through its various ministries. You might be asking, What does ministry have to do with leadership? Ministry has everything to do with leadership. Ministry is what the church does. The church is God's servant in the world. The church is God's voice railing against the injustices that are perpetrated against the weak and defenseless. It is critical that leaders of the church have a clear picture of the church as minister. They must have a fully developed biblical understanding of the church. If the leaders of the church have no biblical and theological understanding of the church, they will not see ministry as a natural part of their faith at work (see James 1:22-27; 2:14-18).

The church exists to preach the gospel of salvation. Jesus is our model in preaching. He came preaching (see Matthew 4:23; Mark 1:14-15, 38). It is through the preaching of the gospel that men and women are brought into a new relationship with God (see Acts 2:39-41; Romans 1:16-17; 1 Corinthians 1:18-24). The church teaches and preaches the Word of God, thereby building up the saints and calling others into relationship with God, through Jesus Christ (see Ephesians 4:11-16). This process of building up the saints is called edification. As the saints are edified, they become better equipped to do the work of the ministry. We are a community of changed people seeking to effect change in others and our world. The church is made up of people who are new creatures in Christ (see 2 Corinthians 5:17; Ephesians 4:24). They may come from inner city communities or middle class neighborhoods. Yet, we are all one in Jesus Christ. As we engage in social ministry, we are able to enlarge our evangelistic efforts. The African American church has a variety of ministries that it is called to do and can do. There are ministries that we must undertake in our communities. Every church can sponsor a tutorial ministry, youth ministry, housing program, health awareness program, financial management program, and bread and food pantry. There are many African American churches that are actively engaged in preaching and teaching the gospel in word and deed. The church where I currently serve is actively engaged in community social ministry through our youth ministry, missionary groups, community outreach programs, food pantry, and bread ministries. Eastside Community Development Corporation and other social ministry activities are all testimonies of our involvement in the community.

In the New Testament we are reminded of the various types of ministries we should engage in. The church has a social ministry (see Matthew 25:31-46), a teaching ministry (see Matthew 28:20), and a preaching and evangelizing ministry (see Luke 10:30, 37). The church carries out this multifaceted ministry through the "gathered and scattered communities."

The church must always be concerned about its mission. Mission is "the total redemptive work of God to establish his kingdom."[14] When we do missions, we are doing the things that demonstrate the love of God to the world. Feeding the hungry, clothing the naked, visiting the sick, ministering to the incarcerated, healing the brokenhearted, opening the eyes of the blind, and lifting the downtrodden are all missions work. Mission takes priority over any phase of church work. Edward H. Hammett has stated that "the church that will survive in the future will be the church that sees itself as a 'missions outpost' from which the gathered church scatters."[15]

There is a difference between doing church work and doing the work of the church. Church work refers to those activities that we engage in to keep the organization alive and vital. Activities that can be included in church work are committee meetings, singing in the choir, serving as an usher in the church--all of these are things that occur within the church building. There is a need for people to engage in church work. The organizational activities of the church must be maintained. However, they are not the real work of the church. The work of the church is the work that Jesus Christ commanded that we do--preach the gospel to those who need to hear good news (see Matthew 28:18-20; Acts 1:8).

The African American church falters in the area of ministry service, missions support and giving. There are literally thousands of African American churches who do nothing in their communities. Very few churches give much more than token support to missions. Missions giving and missions work is an area where we must grow. We must grow in our financial support. We must grow in our commitment to training and sending missionaries to the foreign fields.

The church must respond positively to the divine call of God. We must see ourselves as people on a life and death mission. The concern about mission reflects the seriousness with which the church takes its faith commitment. Eugene L. Stockwell has placed this matter in clear perspective:

> The gathered congregation has one major function, which is the preparation for mission. The scattered congregation has as its main function the participation in mission. Mission is at the very heart of the congregation. All that happens in the gathered life of the congregation is determined by the nature of the mission. All that happens in the scattered life of the congregation is equally determined by the mission.[16]

Thus it appears that if the church is to fully participate in the historical activity of God within the world, it must see its mission clearly, concisely and biblically. We are as the Apostle Paul declared, "Co-laborers with God" (see 1 Corinthians 3:9).

The church is a worshiping community. It seeks to recognize God's presence and Lordship in, and through, its corporate worship experiences. Worship is at the center of what believers are called to do. We are reminded of the importance of corporate gatherings as a time for encouragement and edification (see Hebrews 10:24-25).

As a community, the church offers itself as a servant of the people, meeting human needs wherever they exist, with whatever resources it has available (see Matthew 25:31-46; Acts 11:29; 2 Corinthians 8:1-5; Philippians 2:25; 4:18). As "new creatures in Christ," the church is an evangelizing community, leading men and women to Christ and into fellowship with him (see Acts 8:1-12; 10:44-48; 11:19-21).

The church is a community that must always be concerned with social justice and the dignity of men and women, who have been created in the "image of God." The church of Jesus Christ stands over against every institution that seeks to take advantage of the poor and helpless. The Christian church is a powerful force when it seeks to demonstrate the righteousness of God to an unrighteous world. Its heritage is rich, its mission serious, and its power is unlimited.

The world in which we live is ever evolving. New social and political situations call for new strategies for spreading the gospel. Therefore, the African American church can ill-afford to become complacent but must continue to rise up and meet the contemporary challenges of the post-nuclear age. The goal of a saved world remains! Lindgren stated that "to achieve this goal requires that the first most basic concern of the Church administrator is to have a clear understanding of the nature and purpose of the Church."[17]

The Church must continue to strive for relevance without becoming secular in it's approach to ministry. Bennett remarked that "the Church is not to be a static organization, but a living organism."[18] If the Church is to keep from becoming the victim of its own successes and failures, it must repeatedly reaffirm its purpose, clarify goals, develop and implement plans for spiritual growth, and train and enable new leaders to take hold of the vision of Jesus Christ. Here lies the central concern of the African American Baptist Church, that is, its need for a ready pool of lay leaders who will lead with determination and purpose, making the church a more effective agent of spiritual and social change.

The Church As a System

Systems theory is one of the latest organizational theories to be developed. Lindgren and Shawchuck have noted that systems theory is "the least known and practiced by American religious organizations."[19] Systems theory views the organization as a unified whole which is comprised of various component parts or subsystems. Its central concern is with the "interrelatedness and interdependency" of the organization and its people. Systems theory operates on the assumption that organizational effectiveness is best achieved when the subsystems function together as a single unit, as opposed to operating independently.[20]

The task of church leaders is to lead their individual groups to work cooperatively in achieving the overall mission of the church. Michael C. Mack has written a book in which he proposed integrating small groups into the Sunday School, as a vehicle for enhancing spiritual growth. He stated that when small groups can be forged into working partners, the church can function more effectively. "In other words, when two or more groups work together, they can produce more than they all can independently."[21] A systems understanding allows us to see the total church by looking at its various parts, i.e., auxiliaries, boards, committees and departments.

When we understand the church as a whole system, we can better understand how events can have a rippling effect throughout the church. Whatever happens in one part of the organization has an impact on other parts of the organization. If there is a problem within the Music Ministry, it could spillover into all the choirs and could conceivably create a problem in other parts of the congregation. It is, therefore, reasonable to assume that as the various boards, committees, and auxiliaries work in concert with one another, the entire church functions more effectively.

Biblically, we see the systems approach in Paul's discussion about spiritual gifts in his first letter to the Corinthian church. In 1 Corinthians 12:14, Paul compared the church to a human body. The Corinthian congregation was sharply divided over personalities, wisdom, and the primacy of certain spiritual gifts (see 1 Corinthians 1:10-31; 12:1). Their divisions threatened to wreck the church and destroy the work of Paul's preaching. Paul wanted to show them that the church, while it had many members, was still one single organism. Each part of the body has its own role to play in the smooth functioning of the entire body. The church has many members, but it remains one body. It is the unity of the body that prohibits any one part of the body saying to another part that it has no need of it (verses 15-16). It is the unity of the body that makes each part interdependent upon the next part in order to function properly (verse 17). This became graphically clear to me in January 1998 when I developed something called "Bell's Palsy." It is a temporary paralysis of one side of the face. The nerve that controls that side of the face shuts down and does not work. Without that nerve, I could not control my blinking, chewing, talking, and hearing. The whole left side of my face ceased to work without that nerve. In the church, the body is made up of many different people, but it is only one body.

The key to the success of the systems approach to organizational effectiveness is in the quality of trained lay leadership at the subsystems level. Lay leaders who are knowledgeable of the church's mission and the dynamics of small group interaction and leadership will enhance the overall effectiveness of their various subsystems. When small group leaders are effective in their work, the church will ultimately be successful.

If the local African American Baptist church is going to achieve its worldwide mission of evangelism, it is imperative that it have a theologically and biblically grounded self-understanding. Wherever the leadership of a congregation lacks sufficient knowledge of who they are as the "people of God" and what it means to be "called out of the world," it naturally follows that the local church will be ineffective in carrying out its divine mission. The starting point for developing effective Christian leaders in the local African American Baptist church must begin with a reaffirmation of the nature and purpose of the church as Jesus Christ intended it to be.

Effective lay leaders are not the only ingredient necessary for effective ministry. The church must also develop an organizational structure and understanding that compliments its lay leadership. The systems theory offers the church a foundation upon which to strengthen its ministry and local outreach. It views the church from the standpoint of its wholeness and its intrinsic unity. Each group and its leader are a part of a larger whole, with a corresponding larger mission. Every part of the church works in cooperation with other church parts to achieve the one mission: preaching the gospel of God's salvation to a lost and unredeemed humanity.

Jesus is Head of the Church

No discussion of the church is complete without a discussion of who is the head. Oftentimes men and women want to claim for themselves the position that belongs exclusively to Jesus Christ. I have been to many churches where the traditions and thinking of some church leaders precludes the work of the Holy Spirit within the church. There is a lack of biblical understanding regarding the church's spiritual structure. Practically, we cannot organize the church until we come to understand how the New Testament church organized itself. Our understanding of church leadership is guided by the Scriptures.

The New Testament makes it clear that Jesus Christ, the Resurrected Lord of creation, is the Head of the church. Paul reminded the church at Ephesus that he made constant mention of them in his prayers (Ephesians 1:17). He wanted them to receive a spirit of wisdom and revelation from God (verse 17). Paul wanted the Ephesians to have the understanding of their eyes to be opened to see the greatness of God's glory and calling (verse 8). He wanted them to see the unsurpassing greatness of God's power. And they could see it in Jesus Christ, whom God raised from the dead (verses 19-20). Jesus is the demonstration of the power of God for redemption, healing and reconciliation (see 1 Corinthians 1:18). Jesus has taken the seat of authority at the right hand of the Father in the heavenlies (verse 20). He has power and authority above all rule, authority, power and dominion (verse 21). God has put all things in subjection to Jesus (verse 22a). God has given Jesus to be the head over all things that relate to the church (verse 22b). The church is His body; it is the fulness of Him who fills all in all (verse 23). Curtis Vaughan remarked that Paul made three statements regarding the church's relationship to Jesus.

Three things are emphasized in the figure of Christ's headship over the church: First, He has supreme *authority* over the church; He guides, governs, and controls it. To Him, the church is wholly responsible. Second, a vital *union* exists between Christ and His church, a union as close and real as that of head and body. The relationship of the two is, therefore, intimate, tender, and indissoluble. Third, the church is completely *dependent* upon Christ. From Him it derives its life, its power and all else required for its existence.[22]

Biblically, it is clear that leaders within the church must reckon that their positions are not supreme. There is only one Supreme Head, Jesus Christ. Jesus is the Head of everything and everybody within the church. When we seek to usurp the place of Jesus Christ as Head of the church, we run the risk of ceasing to be the people of God. God, through the Holy Spirit, leads, guides and orchestrates the work and ministry of the church.

Paul went on to describe the church as the body of Christ. In verse 23 we read, "Which is His body, the fulness of Him who fills all in all." The use of the metaphor "body" to describe the church emphasizes the intimate relationship that exists between Christ and the church. Indeed, as Vaughan has stated, "Together they constitute one organism, each, in a sense, being incomplete without the other."[23] In Jesus the church finds its completion. All that is needed to complete its mission successfully is found within the fulness of Christ.[24] Through Jesus Christ, we understand ourselves as the agent of God. Our purpose grows out of our understanding and commitment to His purpose.

Jesus is the "Head of the Church." He is the "chief cornerstone" upon whose shoulders rest the very foundation of the church. In his blood, shed on Calvary, the "new covenant" between God and man is ratified. Without Jesus Christ as Head of the church, there can be no Christian church. Therefore, as Head of the church, Jesus Christ is also head of every organization and auxiliary in the church. It is from Him that small group leaders, under the guidance of the pastor, receive direction.

A Biblical Theology of Leadership

*"... And whoever wishes to be first among you shall
be slave of all."*

Mark 10:44

In the contemporary church, there are all kinds of leaders.
There is a senior pastor with a host of other preachers, deacons,
deaconesses, trustees, musicians, ministry leaders, presidents,
vice presidents, committee chairs, youth sponsors, departments
heads, etc. The list goes on and on. Much of the literature
written on the subject of leadership draws upon contemporary
models and thinking. As I stated previously, there is nothing
wrong with this, provided the starting point for understanding
leadership is with the church. Where, then, does the church look
for leadership training that is spiritual and Christ-centered?

Leadership in the church is different from that found in other
social, political or educational organizations. We cannot stress
this enough. The church is a spiritual organism, called into being
by God to achieve the purposes of God in the world. Therefore,
those who lead are called by God to fulfill God's purpose and not
their own agenda.

In this chapter, we are going to take a look at leadership in the New Testament. Specifically, we want to come to some conclusion as to who were the leaders in the first century Christian church. What were the criteria used to select leaders for the church, and what were their roles? What can we learn about biblical leadership which will help us to develop more effective leaders for our churches today?

The Leadership of Jesus

No discussion of Christian leadership is complete without a consideration of Jesus Christ, the founder and reigning King of the Christian faith. Jesus is the central figure in the New Testament. The story of the New Testament is the story of Jesus Christ. In this section, we will take a look at the leadership of Jesus as a model for our leadership. Why not start with the Old Testament? Because the church is the context of our leadership, therefore, it is only reasonable to see Jesus as the starting point for biblical models. We are members of the church of the Lord Jesus Christ. Jesus is our Leader! We have seen that the church is the product of the intentional work and mission of Jesus. He is the founder of the church (see Matthew 16:18).

The Mission of Jesus

The mission of Jesus is rooted deep within the Old Testament (see Genesis 3:15; Isaiah 53). He came to save a lost and dying humanity from sin. The angel of the Lord told Joseph, "And she will bear a Son; and you shall call His name Jesus, for it is He who will save His people from their sins" (Matthew 1:21; see also, Luke 2:11; John 1:29). The New Testament makes it clear that Jesus came into the world to save sinners (see 1 Timothy 1:15). He came to be a ransom for our sins (Matthew 20:28). Through His death on the cross, Jesus revealed to us the depth of the love of God (see John 3:16; Romans 5:8, 10).

Jesus used several methods to accomplish His mission. **First, He accomplished His mission through preaching the gospel of the kingdom of God (see Mark 1:15-16).** The gospel writers make it clear that Jesus preached. "And He said to them, 'Let us go somewhere else to the towns nearby, in order that I may preach there also; for that is what I came out for'" (Mark 1:38). The African American church thrives on preaching. It is preaching that is at the heart of Black worship. Preachers must realize that leading is one of the tasks associated with preaching. Therefore, preaching must serve as the strategy that is used to bring men and women into a saving relationship with Jesus Christ. Preaching is the means by which we inspire the people of God to do the work of God. Through preaching the church is edified. If preaching is done just to impress the folks and thrill them in worship, then preaching will be empty, shallow and void of any transformative power.

Second, Jesus accomplished His mission through teaching (see Matthew 4:23; 9:35; 13:54; Mark 1:21; 6:2; 10:1; Luke 4:15; 6:6; 13:10; John 6:59). Early in His ministry, Jesus was recognized as someone who taught with authority. "And they went into Capernaum; and immediately on the Sabbath He entered the synagogue and began to teach. And they were amazed at His teaching; for He was teaching them as one having authority, and not as the scribes" (Mark 1:21-22). Jesus' authority was inherent in who He was. He did not need any man or woman to sanction His work. His work was sanctioned by the Father. His teaching helped the masses to discover God in ways they had not before. Jesus' followers learned how to pray, worship God, preach, teach, cast out demons and serve the masses by watching Him.

The African American church has to be concerned about the teaching ministry of the church. There must be concern on two levels. **First**, we must be concerned about what is taught. Does what we teach enrich and increase spiritual growth and ministry effectiveness? What is taught in church or in a training session must make a real difference in the lives of people and in the life of the church. **Second**, we must be concerned about who is teaching. What is the level of knowledge, personal character and public reputation of the teacher? The ministry of teaching is a spiritual gift given to the church for the purpose of building up the church for the work of ministry (see Romans 12:7; 1 Corinthians 12:28-29; Ephesians 4:11; 1 John 3:1). One of the reasons that Jesus was effective and authoritative was because of His personal character. He walked the talk. Jesus was a genuinely spiritual man who did the things necessary to cultivate a deep and meaningful relationship with the Father. Prayer was at the center of Jesus' life. "And it was at this time that He went off to the mountain to pray, and He spent the whole night in prayer to God."

His opponents tried often and unsuccessfully to discredit His name and work. One day, after Jesus had completed a demon exorcism, His detractors began to criticize His work. "But some of them said, 'He cast out demons by Beelzebul, the ruler of the demons'" (Luke 11:15). There was nothing that the opponents of Jesus could find to shame His name. His character was impeccable.

We must be especially concerned that our programs and ministries are designed to train and prepare our leaders for relevant ministry in this millennium. There are far too many African American churches where investment in teaching and training is not done. Training and preparation is one of the most important lessons to be learned from the life of Jesus. An untrained and unprepared church is going to have a difficult time growing in the future.

Third, Jesus used the power of healing to accomplish His mission. Jesus entered a world that was filled with broken and hurting people (see John 5:1). Jesus performed many miracles of healing. He cleansed lepers and cast demons out of the possessed (see Mark 1:40; 5:1-16). Then He healed many who were sick with various diseases and cast out many demons. He did not allow the demons to speak, because they knew Him (Mark 1:34). Even death was no match for the power of Jesus (see Mark 5:35-42; John 11:38-44). In Matthew 4:23-25 there is a summation of the ministry of Jesus and the impact He had upon the lives of people. It serves as a model for any church that wishes to develop a socio-evangelical ministry.

And Jesus was going about in all Galilee, teaching in their synagogues, and proclaiming the gospel of the kingdom, and healing every kind of disease and every kind of sickness among the people. And the news about Him went out into all Syria; and they brought to Him all who were ill, taken with various diseases and pains, demoniacs, epileptics, paralytics; and He healed them. And great multitudes followed Him from Galilee and Decapolis and Jerusalem and Judea and from beyond the Jordan.

Fourth, Jesus accomplished His mission through sacrificial service. Jesus was among the people of His day as a servant. Jesus saw Himself as a Shepherd who had come to give His life for the sheep. "I am the good shepherd. The good shepherd gives His life for the sheep" (John 10:11 NKJV). Jesus came to die for the sins of the world (see John 3:16). His death on the cross made it possible for us to have a new relationship with the Father. Through His sacrifice, we are made whole.

The Leadership Strategies of Jesus

Strategy has been defined by Goodstein, Nolan and Pfeiffer as "a coherent, unifying, and integrative pattern of decisions."[1] By this they mean that strategy development is a deliberate and intentional process. They use the term "proactive."[2] An effective strategy is essential for success.

Robert Dale in his book, *Leading Edge: Leadership Strategies from the New Testament,* put strategic thinking and planning within the context of the church. He wrote, "Strategy is how religious leaders discover, maintain, and enrich the stewardship of their gifts, abilities, and strengths--their edge."[3]   Strategy is what we do to turn our visions into plans and our plans into reality. Without strategy, we are going to have a difficult time being successful.

Aubrey Malphurs wrote, "Strategy is the process that determines how you will accomplish the mission of your ministry."[4] According to Malphurs, this definition has three components. **First**, strategy involves a mission.[5] Mission defines your purpose and direction. **Second**, strategy is a process.[6] This is the process by which we take persons from sinner to saint. **Third**, strategy answers the questions how to, when, who, what, and where?[7] These questions are important because how we are going to accomplish our mission is crucial to developing a direction and a plan to get there.

Strategy has to be realistic and achievable. It would not make any sense to plan to grow your church to 2000 members in a town where only 1000 people live. In order to be achievable, a strategy has to be something that you can reasonably achieve given your situation. Michael Allison and Jude Kaye stated that "strategies are choices about how best to accomplish an organization's mission."[8]   Strategic planning is the belief that our futures can be influenced and changed by what we do now.[9] Jesus used specific strategies to conduct his ministry.   Robert Dale has identified seven strategic activities of Jesus.[10]

- To launch the kingdom of God, Jesus focused on defining himself.

- To launch the kingdom of God, Jesus focused on building a new community.

- To launch the kingdom of God, Jesus focused on training apprentices.

- To launch the kingdom of God, Jesus focused on his selected times and places for action.

- To launch the kingdom of God, Jesus focused on mobilizing his representatives.

- To launch the kingdom of God, Jesus focused on modeling love.

- To launch the kingdom of God, Jesus focused on the risks of success.

The Leadership Model of Jesus

Our study would be incomplete without an examination of the leadership model of Jesus. Jesus epitomizes what we should be as leaders among His people. One of the most difficult task that Jesus faced with His disciples was changing their concepts about true greatness. They believed that greatness was in being the chief among the people and having the seats of power and authority. On several occasions, Jesus had to correct them regarding how they saw leadership.

In Mark 9:33-37 (see also, Mark 10:35-45), there is the account of how Jesus taught the first of many lessons about greatness. As they traveled to Capernaum, they argued among themselves over who was the greatest. They obviously created quite a stir because Jesus asked them what they were discussing along the way (verse 34). He sat down and taught them a lesson on true greatness. If anyone wants to be first, he shall be last of all, and servant of all (verse 35). In the mind of Jesus, the greatest in the kingdom is not the one calling for others to see them, but he who sees himself or herself as a servant of the group. Robert K. Greenleaf states that his ideas about servant leadership came from reading Hermann Hesse's *Journey to the East*.[11]

> In this story, we see a band of men on a mythical journey, probably also Hesse's own journey. The central figure of the story is Leo, who accompanies the party as the *servant* who does their menial chores, but who also sustains them with his spirit and his song. He is a person of extraordinary presence. All goes well until Leo disappears. The group falls into disarray and the journey is abandoned. They cannot make it without the servant Leo. The narrator, one of the party, after some years of wandering, finds Leo is taken into the Order that had sponsored the journey. There he discovers that Leo, whom he had known first as *servant*, was in fact the titular head of the Order, its guiding spirit, a great and noble leader.[12]

Jesus was a servant first. He was not afraid nor too big to stoop and do the most menial of tasks. Greenleaf remarked, "The great leader is seen as servant first, and that simple fact is the key to his greatness."[13] In John 13:4-17, we see Jesus and His disciples celebrating their final Passover meal together prior to His crucifixion. While they were celebrating, Jesus rose from the table, laid aside His garments and wrapped a towel around His waist (verse 4). He took a basin of water, stooped down and began to wash the feet of His disciples (verse 5). Simon did not want Jesus to wash his feet. Jesus told him if He did not wash his feet, Simon would have no part in Him (verse 8). Simon wanted Jesus to wash him all over. The point of the washing was two-fold. **First,** Jesus wanted to demonstrate to His disciples what it meant to be a servant. Definitions are fine, but living examples are clearer. **Second,** when Jesus washed their feet, it was a symbol of spiritual cleansing. Every leader within the church must examine their spirituality. Am I doing the things necessary to develop and maintain a committed and close relationship with the Lord? If you and I expect to be Christlike leaders, we must possess a spirit of humility and service.

Leadership in the Old Testament

The Old Testament is abundant with leaders who led Israel in the direction of God's purposes. Some were successful and some were not. The one major point of similarity among them was their belief that they had been divinely chosen and ordained by God to be the national leader. Whether they were tribal leaders, such as Abraham, or a king and prophet, such as David and Elijah, the fact is clear that God chose them (see Jeremiah 1:5).

The Leadership Model of Moses

The first leader of major significance that one encounters in the Old Testament is Moses. By looking at Moses, I am in no way lessening the prominence of Abraham, chief patriarch of Israel, without whom there would have been no Israel. While a detailed biographical sketch of the life of Moses will not be set forth, there are several points that need to be established about him.

First, and most important, was Moses' belief and conviction that God had specifically chosen him for a particular task of leadership (see Exodus 3:1). Leaders must have a clear sense of calling. God calls us for different purposes and at different times. Moses was called to lead the children of Israel out of the land of their bondage.

Second, Moses did not feel that he was born with any special gifts or recognizable talents. In fact, when called to go to Egypt to tell the Pharaoh to release Israel from bondage, he pointed out his speaking handicaps. "Then Moses said to the Lord, 'Please, Lord, I have never been eloquent, neither recently nor in time past, nor since Thou hast spoken to Thy servant; for I am slow of speech and slow of tongue'" (see Exodus 4:10). He lacked self-confidence.

Third, Moses had the idea that the people would not believe him (see Exodus 4:1-9). "Then Moses answered and said, 'What if they will not believe me, or listen to what I say?' For they may say, 'The Lord has not appeared to you'" (verse 1). During the initial stages of his commission to go to Egypt and lead Israel to freedom, Moses had one assistant, Aaron, who served as his spokesman.

Upon the eventual release of the children of Israel from bondage in Egypt, Moses became the head of the fledgling nation. His task was to mold a group of individual tribes into a single nation and lead them safely to the "promised land." The question that concerns us here is, What did it mean to be head in the Old Testament?

The Hebrew word for "head" (r'osh) has many different usages. The word is used 750 times throughout the Old Testament.[14] Richards and Hoeldtke have pointed out in their study that "individuals could be heads of their families (cf. Exodus 6:14); heads of tribes (cf. 2 Chronicles 5:2); military heads, elected by the elders (cf. Judges 11:11); or they could be progenitors or tribal elders (cf. Numbers 7:12)."[15] There is no question that in the Old Testament the term "head" (r'osh) was applied to human leaders. Their leadership involved an authority that was judicial and/or authoritative.[16]

Moses' Big Blunder

Moses made a crucial mistake in the early days of his tenure as Israel's leader. He tried to do everything by himself. When the burden of leadership became more than one man could humanly bear, Moses, under the advice of his father-in-law, Jethro, appointed assistants to share the workload. Leaders were organized into hierarchies to handle individual problems and concerns.[17] All of the leaders were given a certain level of responsibility and authority. They were to bring major problems to Moses' attention. Under this system, leaders had to possess certain traits, i.e., ableness, reverence for God and honesty (see Exodus 18:21).

It is important to note here that the newly appointed leaders were not just thrown into their positions without preparation for leadership. Moses was to provide training for them in order to enable them to do an effective job (see Exodus 18:20). Leaders were assigned specific tasks and given explicit instructions on how to discharge their duties (cf. Exodus 18:22). It is clear that Moses adopted an enabler form of leadership in which he trained others to assume and share leadership responsibility. Thus, early in the history of Israel, the theological foundation for effective leadership among the people of God was established. One final point. While it is true that Moses was the central figure under this system, God was the Supreme Leader. The initial form of government was a "theocracy" in which God ruled the people.

The Leadership Model of David

A second important leader in the Old Testament was King David. When we think of David, we may have visions of him facing off with Goliath (1 Samuel 17:41-50). We may think of David's spirituality and how he loved God with all of his heart. One might think of David's tragic fall from grace, his sin with Bathsheba, his conspiracy to cover it up and his eventual murder of Uriah (2 Samuel 11). There are many images we have of David in our minds.

When I think of David, I think of one of the most extraordinary leaders in all of history. David's rise to greatness was not the product of his own ingenuity nor ambitions. When Samuel was sent by God to the house of Jesse to anoint Israel's next king, David was the unlikely candidate (see 1 Samuel 16:6-13). It was his openness to God and willingness to be used by God for His purposes that made David a great leader. I would strongly suggest you take the time to read again the life of David in First and Second Samuel. Let's take a look at several of the statements made about David in the Old Testament.

First, David had a keen sense of the calling of God upon his life. He experienced an unusual anointing of the Spirit on the day Samuel anointed him king over Israel. "Then Samuel took the horn of oil and anointed him in the midst of his brothers, and the Spirit of the Lord came mightily upon David from that day forward. And Samuel arose and went to Ramah" (1 Samuel 16:13). The Spirit of the Lord never left David. In spite his faults and glaring sins, David never failed to commune with God. In the darkest moments of his life, he felt that God's presence was with him to offer forgiveness and restoration (see Psalm 51).

Second, David recognized and respected anointed leadership and authority. David knew that Saul was God's chosen vessel. Further, David knew that if he attempted to take Saul's life, he would be in rebellion against the very will of God. Watchman Nee stated that "all things have been created by the authority of God, and all laws on earth are held together through authority."[18] For David to have taken the life of Saul would have been an act of spiritual rebellion against God. "Violating God's authority is a matter of rebellion; it is more serious than violating God's holiness."[19]

When David became a popular hero in Israel, Saul became jealous and pursued David until his dying days (1 Samuel 18:6-8). There were two separate occasions where David had an opportunity to kill King Saul (see 1 Samuel 24 and 26). The first is recorded in 1 Samuel 24. After he returned from pursuing

Israel's arch enemies, the Philistines, Saul received word that David was in Engedi (verse 1). Saul took three thousand of his best soldiers to see if he could capture David. He came to an area known as the "Rocks of the Wild Goats" (verse 2). Near the area called the "sheepfolds," there was a cave. Saul went in to relieve himself, not knowing that David and his men were inside. It was the perfect opportunity for David to get revenge and rid Israel of the leadership of Saul (verse 3).

David's men wanted to kill Saul. "And the men of David said to him, 'Behold, this is the day of which the Lord said to you, behold; I am about to give your enemy into your hand, and you shall do to him as it seems good to you.' Then David arose and cut off the edge of Saul's robe secretly" (verse 4). David's men saw Saul's helplessness as an opportunity to do the will of God; David saw the matter another way.

David rose above what the natural instinct in a man would have him to do. He would not yield to the temptation to take God's prerogatives for judgement into his own hand. His conscience bothered him. It can be safely surmised that the Holy Spirit pricked his heart about touching the very anointed of God. "So he said to his men, 'Far be it from me because of the Lord that I should do this thing to my lord, the Lord's anointed, to stretch out my hand against him, since he is the Lord's anointed'" (verse 6). David had such respect for the king that he would not disrespect him nor allow his men to disrespect Saul, nor God's will.

Third, David loved the Lord with a deep passion. David's love for God was evidenced in his willingness to be obedient and in his spirit of praise. In 2 Samuel 6, shortly after he became king of Israel, David brought the Ark of the Covenant up from the house of Obed-edom (verse 12). As the procession moved along to Jerusalem, David would make a sacrifice every six paces. David rejoiced so much that he came out of his clothes. He danced with all of his might before the Lord (verses 13-14). David had a spirit of praise and worship (see 2 Samuel 7:18-29; 22). Here we see a leader who had no shame in publicly displaying his buoyant love for God.

Lastly, David had a deep love for the people of God. Spiritual leaders must have a deep love for the people whom God has placed him or her over to lead. In 2 Samuel 6:18-19, two important traits are mentioned about David and his relationship to the people. First, after they brought up the Ark of the Covenant and had finished their celebration, David blessed the people in the name of the Lord. Many times leaders of God's people make the mistake of seeing the people as their enemies. There develops an adversarial relationship that thwarts the purposes of God. They are God's people, and the leader needs to learn to respect them and bless them.

The second thing we see in David's attitude toward the people was his willingness to share the spoils of war with them. In verse 19, David gave portions to every one in Israel. Here he showed he had a magnanimous heart and spirit. He cared about those whom he led. These are the things that galvanized the loyalty of the people around him during the dark days of Absalom's rebellion (see 2 Samuel 15:21; 18:1-3). During that dark period in his life, David was considered to be of immeasurable worth to the people of God, even in his old age. Loyalty had been built during the days of David's youth and strength. Leaders must earn the loyalty of those they lead. Church leaders would do well to study the life of David and his relationship with his people.

There are many other worthy examples of leaders in the Old Testament. Among them are Joshua, Nehemiah, Ezra, Hezekiah, Josiah, and the prophets Elijah, Elisha, Isaiah, Jeremiah, Hosea, and Amos. We have only touched the surface of the mighty men and women whom God used to achieve His purposes. All of these men were used by God in significant ways. Their legacies have been preserved in the Scriptures. However, space will not allow for a fuller and more detailed discussion about these notable leaders.

Leadership in the New Testament

The concept of leadership is much different in the New Testament than that found in the Old Testament. The Greek word translated "head" (kephale) refers almost exclusively to a physical head.[13] The church (the people of God) is intimately related to Jesus Christ, as the head is related to the physical body. Thus the concept of leadership in the church is much different than that of other social organizations. Jesus is the head of the body (see Ephesians 1:22; 5:21-30; Colossians 1:18). This lends theological support to the fact that Jesus Christ is the head of every board, committee, and auxiliary in the church.

Within the New Testament, the metaphor of the body is used to describe the church (see Romans 12:4-5; 1 Corinthians 12:12).

This description speaks of the relationship that each member has to one another. Just as various parts of the body are connected to the body, so are individual members connected to the church. These passages describe the interrelatedness and interdependence of the body, thus lending support to the systems approach to church organization. While each member is equally important, there remains the fact that some members are more important by virtue of their function only. You and I can live a relatively normal life without one of our fingers, but we cannot live without a heart.

In the church each member makes a contribution toward the church's effort to minister to the homeless, orphaned, widows, sick, prison bound, and the least of the earth's people. The saints should be encouraged to develop and use their spiritual gifts for ministry. In order to be successful, ministry requires both human and divine leadership.

The work of Richards and Hoeldtke is significant. While there is a distinct difference between the translations of the word "head" from Hebrew to Greek, the basic concepts are the same with regard to meaning and intent. Head refers to the one who is the central leader.

The early church did develop a hierarchial form of leadership with clearly delineated duties and responsibilities (see Acts 6:1; I Timothy 3:3-13). It appears from the New Testament that the organizational structure of the church grew over a period of time and as the need arose for new types of leaders. Whether this was the express intention of Jesus when he called the original twelve disciples to "come and follow him" is not known nor is it the question here. The development of ministry tasks led to a need for ministry leaders. Leadership responsibilities naturally developed following the tremendous growth experienced by the church. In fact, the office that we refer to as deacon had its genesis from the growth of the church.

> Now at this time while the disciples were increasing in number, a complaint arose on the part of the Hellenistic Jews against the native Hebrews, because their widows were being overlooked in the daily serving of food. And the twelve summoned the congregation of the disciples and said, "It is not desirable for us to neglect the word of God in order to serve tables. But select from you, brethren, seven men of good reputation, full of the Spirit and of wisdom, whom we may put in charge of this task. But we will give ourselves to prayer, and to the ministry of the word." And the statement found approval with the whole congregation; and they chose Stephen, a man full of faith and of the Holy Spirit, and Philip, Prochorus, Nicanor, Timon, Parmenas and Nicolas, a proselyte from Antioch. And these they brought before the apostles; and after praying, they laid their hands on them. (Acts 6:1-6)

The apostles were the leaders of the church, and they were assisted in the pastoral care ministry by a group of servants who became the deacons of the church. In Acts 13:1, we are introduced to prophets and teachers, who were a part of the church of

Antioch. We do not know when these two distinct functions first appeared in the church. What is known is that they were present at Antioch. Prophets were men and women who traveled from church to church encouraging and exhorting the infant congregations (see Acts 11:27; 21:9). Teachers were men who moved from church to church. Some who taught the Word of God to the congregation were permanent. Teachers were present in the church. James mentioned that not many of them should strive to be teachers (see James 3:1). Teachers and prophets were listed among the spiritual leadership gifts given to the church by Jesus Christ (see Ephesians 4:11).

Elders in the Church

In Acts 11:30, we are introduced to another leadership office and function, elders. Many churches do not have elders among their core leaders. But as we will see, there appeared to be a distinct difference made between elders and other leaders in the church. The office of elder has its roots in the Old Testament and traditional Jewish religious practice. We must remember that the first disciples of Jesus were all Jewish. It would seem only natural that Jewish synagogues would have elders. Arthur Harrington has noted, "The elder is the most commonly mentioned congregational leader in the New Testament" (Acts 11:30; 14:23; 15:2, 4, 6, 22, 23; 20:17; 1 Tim 5:17, 19; Titus 1:5, 6; 1 Peter 5:1). The second leader most often cited is the deacon (Philippians 1:1; 1 Tim 3:8-12; Romans 16:1).[20]

In Acts 15:2, we see Paul and Barnabas being sent to seek guidance from the apostles and elders of the church at Jerusalem over the question of circumcision. Whoever the elders were, they were not the apostles. Paul instructed Titus to put everything in order and appoint elders in the church (Titus 1:5). He was appointing persons who were to assist him in the ministry at Crete. Obviously, elders served as spiritual leaders in the church who assisted the apostles and pastors. One of the most difficult questions to answer is, Were elders distinct from bishops or pastors? It appears to me that there were people in the church who were called elders, whose function was closely aligned with that of the apostles and pastors.

What we see in Acts is the creation or development of functions of leadership outside of the apostles, namely bishop/pastors, deacons, elders, evangelists, missionaries, bishops, miracle workers, healers, tongue speakers and inter- preters, helpers and administrators.[21] The fact that a hierarchial form of church leadership existed, in no way lessens the spiritual nature and mission of the church. What seems important is that in the New Testament Jesus functioned as the One who empowered and commissioned His followers. The apostles, as He had trained them, ensured the future growth and success of the church.

Functions of New Testament Leadership

Harrington has identified four distinct functions that spiritual leaders in the New Testament performed.[22] Leadership in the New Testament emphasized function more so than position.[23] The primary function that leaders served in the New Testament was empowering the people of God to achieve God's purpose. Moreover, four distinct functions of leaders have been cited:

⇨   **Example**. The first function of leaders was to serve as an example to the flock. They modeled the example of Jesus, who encouraged His disciples to follow Him (see Matthew 8:22; 9:9; 16:24; 19:21; Mark 1:7;2:14; 8:34; Luke 5:27; 9:23, 59; John 1:43; 12:26).

⇨   **Nurture**. Leaders in the church had the responsibility of rearing spiritual infants into mature saints. Nurturing involves all of the functions of spiritual parenting, caring, feeding, protecting, ministering, teaching, and disciplining (see Ephesians 4:14; 1 Corinthians 3:1; 1 Peter 2:2).

⇨   **Equip**. Leaders were charged with the responsibility of preparing the saints for the work of ministry. The church is made up of many functioning parts. When all of these parts work according to their specific function, then the whole body works in a coordinated fashion (see Ephesians 4:12; 1 Timothy 4:6,11,13,16).

⇨   **Service**.   Jesus has called His church to be servants to the world. A primary responsibility of leaders was leading the church to serve others and, especially, those among them. Jesus wanted His disciples to enlist people who were willing to follow His example of service (see Matthew 20:25-28; 25:31-46; John 13: 5-10; Acts 4:32-34; Galatians 6:10).

The church of the twenty-first century should learn a great deal from the teachings of the New Testament. It is through our study of Scripture that we come to know the power and influence of our leadership.

"But select from among you brethren, seven men of good reputation, full of the Holy Spirit and of wisdom, whom we may put in charge of this task."

Acts 6:3

The single, greatest need of the Christian church in the twenty-first century will be for leaders who are filled with the Holy Spirit, wisdom and faith (see Acts 6:3). It will be for men and women who have been born again and have submitted to the authority of the Holy Spirit. The church will need men and women who are spiritually committed to the work of the ministry. J. Oswald Sanders remarked in his classic book, *Spiritual Leadership*, "The overriding need of the church, if it is to discharge its obligation to the rising generation, is for a leadership that is *authoritative*, *spiritual*, and *sacrificial*."[1] Sanders said that authoritative refers to leaders who know where they are going and have the competence to inspire confidence in their followers. The people of God will willingly and freely follow spiritual leaders who lead with the authoritative presence of God upon their lives.

Spiritual leaders recognize that all of their help comes from the Lord (see Psalm 121). Paul reminded the Philippian congregation that he had learned to put total reliance upon the Lord (see Philippians 3:7-9). He had experienced a variety of hardships and joys during his ministry, but through it all, God had made him strong (see 2 Corinthians 11:24-12:10). Spiritual leaders must be built up in Christ because the challenges of ministry can weigh heavily upon them. Paul remarked in Philippians 4:11-13:

Not that I speak in respect from want; for I have learned to be content in whatever circumstances I am. I know how to get along with humble means, and I also know how to live in prosperity; in any and every circumstance I have learned the secret of being filled and going hungry, both of having abundance and suffering need. I can do all things through Him who strengthens me.

What are Spiritual Leaders?

Spiritual leaders are men and women who have been called by God to lead His people; who have been filled and empowered by the Holy Spirit; and who have submitted to His will in all that they do and say. In Acts 6:3, one of the traits sought in the first servants of the church was spirituality, men who were filled with the Holy Spirit. **"But select from among you, brethren, seven men of good reputation, full of the Spirit and wisdom, whom we may put in charge of this task."** The task that is referred to here was the task of looking after the widows of the church and overseeing the widow's fund.

One of the signs of a strong congregation is the presence of people who are all filled with the Holy Spirit and who will live under the authority of God's Word. In the book of Acts, we see how the Holy Spirit empowered and emboldened the saints for serious ministry to their generation. In Acts 4:31 we read, "And when they had prayed, the place where they had gathered together was shaken, and they were all filled with the Holy Spirit, and began to speak the word of God with boldness."

According to J. Oswald Sanders, sacrificial leadership is leadership modeled on the life of Jesus Christ, who gave Himself as a sacrifice for the entire world (see John 1:29; 3:16; Hebrews 9:24-26).[2] It is crucial that leaders in the church today be willing to sacrifice their time, energy, resources, and very lives for the work of the ministry. Leaders, like all believers, are challenged to present themselves as living sacrifices to the Lord to be used in the service of God. The Apostle Paul wrote in Romans 12:1-2:

I urge you therefore, brethren, by the mercies of God, to present your bodies a living and holy sacrifice, acceptable to God, which is your spiritual service of worship. And do not be conformed to this world, but be transformed by the renewing of your mind, that you may prove what the will of God is, that which is good and acceptable and perfect.

Christian leaders are called to give themselves in the mission and ministry of the church. Christian leaders are called to be faithful to the work of the ministry (see 1 Corinthians 4:2). When we present ourselves as living sacrifices, we can lead the people of God to present themselves as living sacrifices for the work of ministry. In 2 Corinthians 8:1-5, Paul wrote of the Macedonians and how they were willing to make great sacrifices for the work of the ministry. But before they could, they had to give themselves to the Lord. Someone in that church led in that effort. Someone in that church motivated the people to submit to God in such a tremendous show of support. Someone modeled submission.

Now, brethren, we wish to make known to you the grace of God which has been given in the churches of Macedonia, that in a great ordeal of affliction their abundance of joy and their deep poverty overflowed in the wealth of their liberality. For I testify that according to their ability, and beyond they gave of their own accord, begging us with much entreaty for the favor of participation in the support of the saints, and this, not as we had expected, but they gave themselves to the Lord and to us by the will of God.

The Dangers of Unspiritual Leadership

What happens when the church is saddled with leaders who are not lovers of nor seekers after the will of God? What happens to the people of God when the leaders are carnal and self-seeking? What happens to the people of God when the leaders seek not to serve but to be served? What happens to the ministry of the church when the leaders are neither interested in nor knowledgeable of the mission and purpose of the church? What happens to the church when the leaders are more interested in titles and positions than they are in the functions of their positions? When the church's leaders are unspiritual, everything in the church suffers. The people, mission, stewardship, outreach, giving, growth, teaching, preaching, service, ministry, and worship all suffer when there is unspiritual leadership in the church.

Unspiritual leaders refuse to submit to the authority of the Word of God, the leadership of the Holy Spirit, and the pastor. Unspiritual leaders are a liability to the church, and they will only produce followers who, like themselves, are rebellious, spiritually bankrupt, disobedient, and worldly-minded (see Numbers 16:1).

One of the constant problems that the disciples of Jesus had was their focus on seats of prominence and power within the kingdom of God (see Mark 10:37). They saw Jesus as the One who could give them the recognition that they have did not and could not find elsewhere. Their concept of the kingdom of God was narrow and self-centered. James and John alienated other members of their fellowship by seeking chief seats without understanding the enormous commitment that came with such kingdom prominence (see Mark 10:35-45).

Ineffective leadership is not difficult to detect. Jesus said that false prophets would not be difficult to identify (see Matthew 7:15-16). Joe S. Ellis has identified six symptoms that indicate a lack of effective leadership within the church. These problems are not doctrinal nor philosophical in nature, rather they stem from a lack of spiritual understanding regarding the real nature of the church and the dynamics of group behavior and leadership. Further, we can rightly assume that they point to a problem of spiritual immaturity on the part of church leaders. We must begin to address this concern in significant ways.

1. Poor interpersonal relationships among members or between members and those in offices. Inability of people to understand each other, friction, conflict, criticism, and general lack of ability to get along with each other--to say nothing of working together productively.

2. Aimlessness or inertia. Inability of people to rally to a common direction or purpose.

3. Puzzling attitudes and behaviors among the members. Unjustified demands or expectations for the church or minister. Inadequate views of their own roles as Christians in the congregation.

4. Ineffective programs, irrational policies, pointless routines, or useless traditions that defy efforts to change them.

5. Low morale, lack of motivation, indifference, irresponsibility, pessimism, and poor cooperation (indicated by low attendance, inadequate finances, lack of workers).

6. Preoccupation with trivial details to the neglect of the primary responsibilities of the church.

All of these problems are symptoms of failure in the role of purpose. This, in turn, reflects a need for leaders who understand the nature of the church, the principles of working with people, and the principles of effective leadership.[3]

Five Traits of Unspiritual Leadership

1. Unspiritual leaders lead the people of God astray and into sinful acts (Exodus 32:1-7).
2. Unspiritual leaders exhibit and lack faith in the promises of God (Numbers 13:32-33).
3. Unspiritual leaders will seek to lead rebellions against the set leader of God's people (Numbers 16:1-4).
4. Unspiritual leaders deceive God's people for their own personal gain (Judges 9:26).
5. Unspiritual leaders rebel against the commandments of God (1 Samuel 15:1).

Let's take a closer look at the nature of spiritual leadership. It is important that we begin to see some of the principles of spiritual leadership that will better assist us in doing our jobs as leaders within the church of God.

The Nature of Spiritual Leadership

The Christian life is first and foremost a life of commitment to the teachings and mission of Jesus Christ. It is life lived in submission to the power of the Holy Spirit. The Christian life is life in the Spirit, which makes us spiritual. The Holy Spirit is both the Agent of our salvation and the Source of our power (see Acts 2:1-4; 37-47). All believers who profess Jesus Christ as their Lord and repent of their sins, in faith, receive God's gift of the Holy Spirit (see 1 Corinthians 12:7). He dwells in us for the benefit of building up the body of Christ, the church.

Believers are called to live under the dominion of the Holy Spirit (see Romans 8:11-14). In Jesus Christ, God has given us a new nature which replaced our old nature of sin, which leads to death and destruction. Paul wrote in Ephesians 4:23-24, "And that you be renewed in the spirit of your mind, and put on the new self, which in the likeness of God has been created in righteousness and holiness of the truth."

The appointment and anointing of persons to be leaders is one of the gifts that the Holy Spirit gives to the church (see Romans 12:8). Paul wrote to the Corinthians, "And God has appointed in the church, first apostles, second prophets, third teachers, then miracles, then gifts of healings, helps, administrations, [and] various kinds of tongues" (1 Corinthians 12:28 NASB). The spiritual gift of leadership is the divinely given capacity to guide, direct and superintend the ministry of the local church. God establishes leaders at all levels of the church's life, even denominational leadership is a gift from God. Paul directed Titus to lead a group of congregations on the island of Crete. While there, he was also directed to appoint elders in every city. "For this reason I left you in Crete, that you might set in order what remains, and appoint elders in every city as I directed you ... " (Titus 1:5; Acts 15:1-31). In Ephesians 4:11-12, we are told that God has placed some offices within the church for the express purpose of building up the body of Christ and for the work of the ministry.

Spiritual leaders are not elected, voted upon, nominated, nor appointed by the church, rather they are called by God to serve His purposes and people (see Exodus 3:1; Numbers 27:15-23; Joshua 1:1-10; Judges 4:4; Isaiah 6:1; Jeremiah 1:1-9; Amos 7:14-15; Luke 5:1-10; Acts 13:1). The church, governed by the Holy Spirit, must consider new ways to select its leaders. There has never been an occasion when God commanded the people to vote on who He wanted to lead His people. Only God can make a man or woman a spiritual leader. There is no amount of training nor preparation that can prepare you for being a spiritual leader in the church today. Leadership begins, first, with a relationship with Jesus Christ and a call to serve. Arthur Harrington has observed:

Church leadership must be conceived as being neither self-made nor congregation-made. In fact, leaders cannot be created by either election or appointment. They are the product of the activity of the Holy Spirit working within their lives. Upon the basis of the visible evidence of this activity, they are to be selected for leadership in Christ's church.[4]

Let's take a few minutes to examine the nature of spiritual leadership. By looking at some of the principles established in the Scriptures, we can begin to develop a new and fresh perspective about biblical leadership.

First, spiritual leadership has its origin in God. Just as the church has its origin in God, so do those who lead God's people. Throughout the Bible, God called men and women to lead His people. Spiritual leaders are called for a specific purpose or function. Moses was called to lead Israel out of slavery in Egypt (see Exodus 3:1). Joshua was chosen and anointed by God to succeed Moses and lead the children of Israel across the Jordan River into the promised land (see Numbers 27:15-23; Joshua 1:1-10). Aaron and his sons were consecrated to lead the children of Israel in worship and celebration of Israel's religious feasts and holy days (Exodus 29:1-20; Leviticus 8).

During the New Testament era, God called and anointed people for specific purposes. In the New Testament, the word "spiritual" is used to designate those people, gifts, places, or things that have their origin in God. Everything that the church does and is, is by its very nature, spiritual.

The New Testament does not provide for a specific leadership organizational structure. The New Testament provides a spiritual blueprint that presents us with guidelines that are to be used in the selection of spiritual leaders for the church. Leaders are responsible for empowering the church to carry out its mission of evangelism, discipleship and edification.

Second, spiritual leadership takes place within the context of the gathered fellowship of God's people. The fact that our leadership is exercised among the people of God, in the house of God, makes it uniquely different and holy. Our leadership is exercised under the anointing presence and power of the Holy Spirit. The gift (individuals such as pastors/teachers) of leadership is specifically given as a gift to the congregation and should be used to build up God's people who do God's work (see 1 Corinthians 12:7, 28; Ephesians 4:11). It is the pastor and spiritual leader's responsibility to ensure that the members are built up spiritually and are prepared to do the work of ministry.

Third, spiritual leadership seeks the successful accomplishment of God's purpose on the earth. Spiritual leaders seek to do the greater works that Jesus called us to (see John 14:12). Spiritual leadership has no agenda, program, ministry, nor vision that is not first given by God. The purpose of God is the reconciliation of the world unto Himself (2 Corinthians 5:19). Spiritual leaders must be committed to the mission of God (see Matthew 28:19-20).

Fourth, spiritual leadership is dynamic leadership. It is dynamic because it is leadership that is energized by the Holy Spirit, who gives spiritual power to the saints of God (see John 15:5; Acts 1:8, 2:4; 2 Corinthians 4:7; Ephesians 6:10). It is the Holy Spirit, who gives us the power to do this work of ministry. Without His presence and power, we would not be able to hold up under the stresses of leadership in this technological age. When leaders and congregations are not true to the biblical purpose of the church, they loose the right to exercise God's power and presence in their midst.

Spiritual Leadership Defined

Let's come to the definition of spiritual leadership. I am going to use the definition of Christian leadership developed by Kenneth O. Gangel as our working definition for spiritual leadership. **"It is the exercise of one's spiritual gifts under the call of God to serve a certain group of people in achieving the goals God has given them toward the end of glorifying Christit."[5]** The key point that I want you to get here is that spiritual leaders use what God has given them for God's purposes with God's people.

Everyone who leads within the church of the Lord Jesus Christ, in any capacity, is called to function as a spiritual leader. For some reason, we have identified as leaders, only the persons who have been duly nominated and voted on by the church. Leaders can be people who have a one time function, such as serving on the annual budget committee. These are clearly very important leadership positions, because these are the persons who help set the course for the church in the coming year. All leaders in the church are spiritual leaders. We are all sanctified through the work of the Holy Spirit, who produces within us the fruit of righteousness, obedience and godliness (see 1 Peter 1:2, 13-16). Paul reminded the Galatian's congregation that the Holy Spirit produces within us readily identifiable evidences that he said were like fruit. "But the fruit of the Spirit is love, joy, peace, patience, kindness, goodness, faithfulness, gentleness, self-control; against such things there is no law" (Galatians 5:22-23). The fruit of the Holy Spirit have to do with our inner lives and the depth of our relationship with the Lord. As leaders, we are to constantly allow the Holy Spirit's fruit to shine and manifest themselves through our words and actions.

Regardless of what your role in the church may be--Sunday School teacher, youth worker, deacon, deaconess, trustee, committee chairperson, ministry leader or member--whatever your position, you are a spiritual leader. In the church, all leaders are spiritual! Spiritual leaders have but one goal: the building up of the body of Christ to do the work of ministry (see Ephesians 4:12-16).

Duties of Spiritual Leaders

"In this case, moreover, it is required of stewards that one be found trustworthy."

1 Corinthians 4:2

What do spiritual leaders do? What role do they play in the church's ministry? Leaders primarily provide direction to the efforts of people. Spiritual leaders provide direction for the work of God's people in ministry. Leaders make the difference in an organization. Joe Ellis remarked in his book, ***The Church On Purpose: Keys To Effective Church Leadership***:

When progress is being made or success achieved, somebody is causing it. Inertia can just happen, but movement is caused. When a church is alive, effective, and progressing, it means that somebody is emphasizing, clarifying, and reminding people of their purpose; somebody is keeping objectives in the spotlight; somebody is showing people how to merge their efforts to accomplish their common goals; somebody is challenging and inspiring others. In other words, somebody is leading. Leadership is the key to effective congregations.[1]

Spiritual leadership is the key to developing congregations that have a keen spiritual focus and orientation on the things that matter most to God. Effective congregations are led by leaders who are focused, intentional, spiritual, and effective. Churches need leaders who will put the work of the kingdom at the center of their agendas. Spiritual leaders give the church the people resources necessary to achieve the mission and vision of the church.

One of the primary tasks of spiritual leaders is to be spiritual. Spirituality is central to Christian character. Without spiritual character we become "sounding brass and tinkling cymbals." In many churches today, we have forgotten that spirituality is developed, and then it must be tended to. We lose the source of our power and authority when we fail to practice spiritual discipline. Norman Shawchuck and Roger Heuser in their book, *Leading The Congregation*, have given this definition of spirituality:

Spirituality is the means by which we develop an awareness of the presence of the loving Lord in our lives, and the processes by which we keep that awareness alive and vital, to the end that we become formed in the Spirit of Christ.[2]

There are many church leaders who are so consumed with doing ministry that they forget to take care of themselves spiritually. They spend little, if any, time in consecrated prayer and study of the Scriptures. We cannot get so caught up in our work that we forget to make time for the Scriptures to shape our ministries. We must remember that doing ministry is not spirituality.[3] As Shawchuck and Heuser stated, "Spirituality is being formed in the nature of Christ and patterning one's life after the example of Christ."[4] They stated further that "spirituality is paying attention to the life of the Spirit within."[5] Spiritual leaders allow the Holy Spirit to manifest His fruit in their lives: love, joy, peace, patience, kindness, generosity, faithfulness, gentleness, and self-control (see Galatians 5:22-23).[6]

One of the ways that leadership has been studied is by examining and identifying what effective leaders do. This method of studying leadership has been called the "trait theory." The premise was, "If you want to learn how to be an effective leader, look at what they do and model that behavior." I want to lay out several behavioral tasks that God's Word identifies with effective spiritual leadership.

Duties of Spiritual Leaders

1. Prepare God's people for effective ministry (Ephesians 4:12; Exodus 18:20-21).

2. Organize God's people for service (Nehemiah 3; Exodus 18:21-22).

3. Inspire God's people with God's immeasurable possibilities through a realistic and achievable vision (Nehemiah 2:17; Ephesians 3:20).

4. Motivate God's people to give the resources necessary for kingdom work (1 Chronicles 29:1-10).

5. Prepare the next generation to serve and obey God (Deuteronomy 6:6; Joshua 4:6; Judges 2:10).

6. Model behavior that is morally and ethically pure (Titus 2:7-8).

7. Nurture and develop disciples (Acts 2:41).

8. Cultivate and develop other spiritual leaders for the ministry (Numbers 11:16).

9. Model the spiritual disciplines by practicing them publicly and privately (Luke 11:1).

10. Acknowledge the Lordship of Jesus Christ (Luke 6:46).

Spiritual Leadership and Teamwork

One of the most important measures of spiritual leadership effectiveness is whether or not the leader was able to get God's people to work together as a team. A team of average players can be very effective when they combine their efforts and work on a common goal. It does not matter how brilliant you are, nor whether or not you have multiple talents, you will need other people in order to achieve your church's mission. Getting people to work together as a team will be one of the most important leadership measures of your success as a leader. We can be much more effective when we can create a climate of participation and cooperation among those whom we lead. In the Old Testament, no one was more effective at getting God's people to work together than Nehemiah. He was able to galvanize the efforts of various groups of people around the goal of rebuilding the walls of Jerusalem (see Nehemiah 3).

Whenever the ministry of a group (or the entire church) revolves around a single person, there exists the potential for ministry disaster. Ministry is much more effective when the saints are enlisted to work together as a team. Teams are more productive because the individual members can give support to other team members. Teams are much more effective than single individuals working alone. One of the biggest problems that Moses had as a new leader was his belief that he was the only one who could perform his tasks (see Exodus 18:7-13). There is always the temptation to want to do things ourselves, without including others in the process. No one person within a group has all of the knowledge and ability to make a group successful in its work. Frank Damazio says that there are ten problems with leadership by a single person.[7]

1. One man cannot successfully shepherd a large flock of God.
2. One man is limited in his ministry and gifts.
3. One man may fail in wisdom, knowledge and judgment.
4. One man will have difficulty in finding the mind of God for everything.
5. One man limits the potential growth.
6. One man has no one to adjust or correct him.
7. One man has no "checks and balances."
8. One man may break physically, mentally, emotionally and morally under pressure.
9. One man may become an autocrat or dictator.

10. One man ministry is contrary to the revealed will of God in the Scriptures, which teach plurality of leadership as well as being "first among equals."

Duties of Spiritual Leaders to the Church

Some of the most important questions that elected and appointed leaders must ask are, What are my responsibilities to the church? What are my responsibilities to the people that I lead? Further, leaders must continue to seek direction for their work from the church. Leaders should also ask these questions: Are there any expectations that the church should have and does have of me as one of its spiritual leaders? Does the church have a right to expect that I will be supportive of the pastor and his/her vision for the church? Does the church have a right to expect that I will lead with compassion and concern for those who follow me? Does the church have a right to expect that I will seek to grow and become competent in my area of ministry? Does the church have a right to expect that I will submit to the authority of God's Word and follow the leadership of the Holy Spirit? Does the church have a right to expect me to demonstrate godly behavior? What does the church have a right to expect of me as a spiritual leader in the church of Jesus Christ?

I have listed several general duties that apply to every leader in the church and some specific ways that these can be exercised. Congregations should begin to define what it believes to be the general obligations of its spiritual leaders. Every responsible spiritual leader should subscribe and submit to these general duties in the church of the Lord Jesus Christ.

1. **Follow the leadership of the pastor.**
   a. Support his/her vision for the future.
   b. Support the church's ministry.
   c. Follow his teaching of the Word.
   d. Respect the biblical role of the pastor.
   e. Submit to the leadership authority of the pastor.

2. **Support the mission, ministry, purposes, and programs of the church.**
   a. Learn the mission statement of the church and teach it to others.
   b. Give freely of your resources and time in support of the church.
   c. Offer to render service where and when needed.

3. **Lead their organizations toward ministry involvement and participation.**
   a. Conduct training on missions and ministry.
   b. Encourage missions giving and evangelism.
   c. Seek ways to involve your followers in ministry and missions.
   d. Solicit ministry suggestions from the pastor.

4. **Work to promote peace, unity, and cooperation among church groups and members.**
   a. Promote positive pastoral images.
   b. Promote positive images of church programs.
   c. Promote internal group peace and unity.
   d. Promote interdependence among other church groups.
   e. Submit to the authority of elected and appointed church leaders.

5. **Embrace and foster the pastor's vision for the future ministry of the church.**

    a. Allow the Lord to build your spiritual eyesight.

    b. Lead others in developing spiritual vision.

    c. Be committed to the future growth of the church.

    d. Express confidence in God's possibilities.

    e. Motivate your followers to embrace the vision.

    f. Be open to change and new ways of thinking and acting.

    g. Become a student of change and its processes.

6. **Build teamwork and team spirit among the members of their group.**

    a. Become a team player and team member.

    b. Promote teamwork and team problem solving.

    c. Seek to resolve conflict immediately.

    d. Value those whom God has given you to lead.

    e. Seek to build team spirit and group identity.

7. **Encourage participation in Bible Study, Prayer Meeting, and Sunday School.**

    a. Commit yourself to developing a deeper spiritual life.

    b. Recognize the power of God's Word.

    c. Use the spiritual resource of prayer in meetings.

    d. Designate specific times for group prayer.

    e. Lead in Sunday School attendance.

    f. Lead the group in discovering their individual spiritual gifts.

    g. Personally practice prayer and Bible Study.

    h. Spend time in meetings discussing God's Word.

8. **Be faithful in their service to the church.**

    a. Make every effort to attend major church functions.

    b.   Encourage people you lead to support church events.

    c.   Seek to exhibit a humble and cooperative spirit.

    d.   Discover ways to work with other church leaders.

    e.   Become committed to biblical stewardship and giving.

    f.   Conduct a Bible study on service and commitment.

9.   **Encourage members of their groups to nurture and use their individual spiritual gifts.**

    a.   Identify and share your spiritual gifts with the group.

    b.   Conduct a Bible study of spiritual gifts.

    c.   Help group members identify their individual spiritual gifts.

    d.   Talk about spiritual gifts in your meetings.

10. **Support and show love for the pastor. He/She needs your help.**

    a.   Spend time each day in prayer for the pastor.

    b.   Be sensitive to the pastor's need for spiritual development.

    c.   Never be the source nor cause of church conflict or rumors.

    d.   Promote the work of the pastor.

    e.   Ask the Holy Spirit how you can minister to the pastor's needs.

    f.   Show love and kindness to the pastor's spouse and family.

Ten Principles of Service for Church Leaders

1.   Leaders must ensure that God is first in everything they do.

2.   Leaders must continuously look for ways to improve the church and its ministry.

3.   Leaders must make sure that everything is done to

the glory of God and to the highest standard of excellence and quality.

4. Leaders must make sure that the members are always first in their actions.

5. Leaders must continuously train and educate themselves in the work of ministry.

6. Leaders must never make excuses for not doing their jobs.

7. Leaders must always take the concerns of the members seriously.

8. Leaders must ensure that new members are taken care of and not deserted.

9. Leaders must be willing to serve the Lord and the church at all times.

10. Leaders must make the kingdom work their number one priority.

The Ministry of the Pastor

"But we will devote ourselves to prayer, and to the ministry of the word."

Acts 6:4

What is the ministry of the pastor? What is the leadership role of the pastor? What are the administrative responsibilities of the pastor? What do the Scriptures report about the pastoral ministry? What is the relationship of the pastor to the church? In this chapter, we want to try to set the stage for answering these questions. These are very important questions that must be asked, as we seek the development of a theologically and biblically sound understanding of the church. God has called and sent the pastor to lead and feed His people.

The word "pastor" denotes images of someone who cares for the flock and shelters it from danger. Jesus told Peter that his primary responsibility would be to feed the sheep and lambs of the Father (see John 20:15-17). The ministry of the pastor is a distinct and specific calling. The pastor receives a calling from God to the ministry, then to the ministry of shepherding. The pastor is the primary leadership and ministry gift given to the church by God. Paul wrote of the gifts given to the church: "And

He gave some as apostles, and some as prophets, and some as evangelists, and some as pastors and teachers, for the equipping of the saints for the work of service, to the building up of the body of Christ" (Ephesians 4:11-12).

Within the Baptist church, the pastor is one of the two primary spiritual leadership functions. The other is the position of deacon/deaconess (see 1 Timothy 3:1). The pastor is the first leader in the hierarchy of church leadership. In his letter to the church at Philippi, Paul addressed the saints, then the leaders of the congregation. "Paul and Timothy, bond-servants of Christ Jesus, to all the saints in Christ Jesus who are in Philippi, including the overseers and deacons" (Philippians 1:1). The pastor is the primary servant leader among many leaders within the church.

The Scriptures clearly teach that the pastor is the primary spiritual leader among the people of God. One of our models for the shepherd/spiritual leader is Moses (see Exodus 18:7-27). Jethro, the father-in-law of Moses, watched his solo leadership. He called him aside and gave him some sound advice on how to lead a large group of God's people. His task was to bring the concerns of the people before the Lord (see Exodus 18:19). Moses was to teach God's Word and show them how to live for God and the work that they were to do (Exodus 18:20). He was told to select, from among the people, able men, men who feared God, men of truth, and men who were honest (Exodus 18:21). They were to take some of the burden off of Moses by taking care of the minor tasks, but the major things they were to bring before him. The pastor is the leader of many leaders in the church.

The function and position of the pastor is divinely ordained by God. "And He gave some as apostles, and some as prophets, and some as evangelists, and some as **pastors and teachers**, for the equipping of the saints for the work of service, to the building up of the body of Christ" (Ephesians 4:11-12). God has set the pastor in the church according to His own pleasure. When God sets a pastor in a congregation, that congregation's work will prosper as it follows his or her leadership. In Revelation 1:12-16, the pastor is referred to as the "angel of the church." The angel of the Lord is the one who delivers the message of God to His people (see Matthew 1:20; Luke 9:52; Revelation 5:2). The word pastor *(poimen)* means shepherd and includes the concept of teaching and preaching. The way to understand the role of the pastoral office is to see it in its biblical context. Our goal is to understand how the Word of God defines the pastoral function.

Qualifications for the Pastoral Office

The Scriptures lay out specific qualifications of the pastoral function. Let's take a look at them.

- ◆ He must be born again and led by the Holy Spirit, Romans 8:12-14.
- ◆ He must manifest the fruit of the Spirit, Galatians 5:22-23; 1 Timothy 6:11; 2 Timothy 2:22.
- ◆ He must have a clean and exemplary life, 1 Timothy 4:12; 5:22; Titus 2:7-8.
- ◆ He must be a diligent student of the Word of God, 2 Timothy 2:15.
- ◆ He must be willing to find contentment in his work, Philippians 4:11-13; 1 Timothy 6:3-5.

- He must be willing to avoid useless and divisive arguments, 1 Timothy 6:3-5.
- He must be committed to conscientiously persevering in his ministry, his message and his personal growth, 1 Timothy 4:15-6; 6:11-20; 2 Timothy 4:3-5.
- He must be willing to equip and empower others for the work of the ministry, Ephesians 4:11-12.

Functions of the Pastoral Office

- The pastor must ensure that he nurtures his personal spiritual growth.
- The pastor must ensure that other church leaders seek to grow and develop spiritual maturity, manifesting the fruit of the Holy Spirit.
- The pastor must be willing to submit to the authority of God's Word and the leadership of the Holy Spirit.
- The pastor must be willing to strive to ensure that church bylaws are properly developed and followed. He should ensure that other leaders and members adhere to the church's rules and orders of discipline. However, he or she must never allow the Bible to be relegated to second class status or to man-made rules.
- The pastor is the congregation's overseer. The overseer is the person responsible for the entire operation. This does not mean that the overseer does everything, rather it means that he is responsible for ensuring that things are done properly (see 1 Timothy 3:1; Acts 20:28).
- The pastor protects the church from false teaching and false teachers (see Acts 20:29-31).

- ◆ The pastor is God's watchman, who watches over the church's spiritual life (see Ezekiel 33:6-7; 2 Corinthians 5:18-20).

- ◆ The pastor is called to point men and women to the truth found in God's Word (see 1 Timothy 4:6).

- ◆ The pastor is to teach the Word of God (see 1 Timothy 4:11).

- ◆ The pastor is an example to the flock (see 1 Timothy 4:12).

- ◆ The pastor is to see that the Scriptures are publicly read, exhort the congregation and teach the Word (see Timothy 4:13).

- ◆ The pastor is to provide general spiritual oversight to the entire congregation (see 1 Timothy 5:1).

- ◆ The pastor preaches the Word to the congregation (see 2 Timothy 4:2).

The Contemporary Leadership Role of the Pastor

What does it mean to be a preacher/prophet/pastor in the infant years of the twenty-first century? Will the role of the preacher change in this millennium? What will the landscape of ministry look like for the African American church, and how will the pastor function within it? It goes without saying that the pastoral task of the preacher is becoming increasingly more demanding. The very nature of the church demands much from the pastor in this generation. Those whom we are called to lead often place enormous expectations upon us.

Things have changed markedly since I entered the pastoral ministry in 1980. When I began my first pastorate, the congregation consisted of 120 worshipers. My wife and I, and our two daughters, lived in Kilmarnock, Virginia, a small, rural fishing and farming community. My biggest responsibility during the week was to prepare a sermon to preach and occasionally visit the sick and shut-in members. Other than that, there were no real pressing demands on my time. Today, with a congregation of nearly one thousand members and all of the other responsibilities, the pastoral ministry is much more demanding and stressful. There are demands from every quarter of the preacher's life. He or she is a family, community, and church person, but most of all, a Christian.

There are days and weeks when there seems to be no end to the demands. There was a time in my ministry when I felt that social and civic involvement was indicative of an effective ministry. It would be great to have this civic involvement on your resume. I serve on several community boards--the Board of Visitors for Norfolk State University and the Urban League--and there are some others that I do not have time to attend. In addition to the civic responsibilities, I serve as president of my state convention, which places me on the board of directors of the national convention. The work of the state convention is very demanding and time consuming. All of these activities require time and have their own host of tasks and responsibilities. Tack on all of the unrelated tasks and distractions that the preacher has through various organizations, and you can end up meeting yourself coming and going. All of these other involvements are things that claim time that could be better spent in ministry, prayer, or study. The pastoral ministry is a big job today. And it requires nearly all of your time and attention.

I want to suggest, and it is not a new revelation, that there is no calling, profession or vocation that is more crucial to the spiritual and social well-being of our culture today than the Christian ministry. While some people want to dismiss the role of the church, particularly the preacher, as irrelevant, it still pleases God through the foolishness of preaching to save the lost (see 1 Corinthians 1:18-21). This is particularly true for the African American community. The church and the preacher are at the center of community life. Like the prophet of old, the preacher stands in the gap between a loving heavenly Father and a wilful and sinful humanity. The preacher is called by God to be God's spokesperson to a world that would rather turn a deaf ear to His will, Word, and ways. The preacher is called to lead the people of God to a more consecrated lifestyle and to fulfill their ministries and calling. God called Jeremiah to speak to his generation about the ills of that day (see Jeremiah 1). Jeremiah was told by God that he was appointed by God "to pluck up and to break down, to destroy, to overthrow to build and to plant" (Jeremiah 1:10b).

The preacher is called by God to stand apart from culture, yet be a participant of culture to challenge culture to higher standards of moral, social, economic, political, and spiritual behavior. We are called to remind the people of God of who they are and why God has called them into relationship with Him. God calls the preacher/pastor to lead from a spiritual center.

The preacher has always had an awesome responsibility! The preacher is responsible to no one but God for how his or her ministry is carried out. The preacher is responsible to society, only to the extent that he or she lives in society and is, therefore, responsible for what men and women see in the preacher's life and obedience to the laws and governing authorities (see Romans 13:1-3).

A Portrait of the Twenty-First Century Pastor/Church Leader

What does a new millennium, African American pastor look like. Pastors will need to possess an array of skills if they are going to be effective in this new millennium. The world in which we live has experienced dramatic, almost cosmic changes, and those who lead the people of God will need to be men and women who are able to adapt and change. I do not mean change our message and moral standards; rather, we must change our methods of doing ministry. Church leaders in this new millennium will need to be agents of change and organizational renewal. It is clear that church structures of the future will need to look much different than they do presently. They will need to be more dynamic and ministry focused, and less institutionalized and corporate. Many churches are still using organizational models that were developed 30, 40, 50, 60 years ago. Pastors will have to become more open to organizational change and development.

Change is the only constant, everything else is in fluid motion. Leaders in the twenty-first century will need to be persons who understand how to effectively bring about change. In 1 Chronicles 12:32, when the Israelites came to Hebron to make David king, there were leaders from the tribe of Issachar who knew and understood the times. "And of the sons of Issachar, men who understood the times, with knowledge of what Israel should do ..." Clearly pastors will need to be men and women who understand the times and who know what should be done. Pastoral leaders must have a clue as to what is taking place religiously, politically, economically, and socially.

In many cases, pastors today are leading churches that are bound to their pasts, which severely limits and restricts their progress. The future is where life will be lived out. The past is where we have been, and we can no more go back in time than we can increase the size of our stature by willing it so. Norman Shawchuck and Roger Heuser pointed out in their book, *Leading the Congregation*, "The only congregations that will thrive in the coming decades will be those whose leaders have learned to *respond* to change, not *resist* or *ignore* it."[1] Therefore, I believe that future church leaders will need to possess certain skills and abilities. I want to suggest what I believe to be the skills necessary for twenty-first century leadership.

Visionary

What is a visionary? A visionary is someone who is able to articulate a significant, meaningful and attractive future for their church, para-church organization, association or state convention. A visionary hears the sounds of the future coming like a man, with his ear on the track, listening for the sound of an approaching train. Visionaries grasp the future by under-standing the present realities. He or she is able to create within the minds of their followers, a picture of a bright tomorrow and how to get there. When God led Nehemiah to go to Jerusalem and lead in the rebuilding of the walls, he said God had put something in his heart and he did not reveal it (see Nehemiah 2:12). What was it that God put in his heart? It was a vision of the walls rebuilt around Jerusalem and life returned to normal.

Vision is a clear picture of tomorrow and how to get there. How does a pastor or spiritual leader develop vision? It begins with having a deep and abiding relationship with God. You cannot have a godly vision without a godly relationship. Vision is the result of being spiritually connected to God according to God's design. There are things that God reveals to us by His Spirit: "For the Spirit searches all things, even the depths of God" (1 Corinthians 2:10). I believe that a vision for the church comes from God and that it is a spiritual revelation of God's intention and direction for a specific group of people at a particular point in history. We have received the Spirit of God, who opens up God's complete will and purpose for our congregations.

Strategic Planner

What is a strategic planner? Congregational leaders will need to be men and women who can think through the steps for achieving a specific purpose or objective. A strategic planner is someone who understands the spiritual, social, economic, and political environment, and all of the competitive forces at work, and devises a plan of action to grow the organization, while maintaining its competitiveness and viability. Strategic planning is a step-by-step process detailing how you intend to achieve God's purpose through your church. Church leaders must plan today for where the Lord wants them to be in the future. What does the future of your church look like? Is there a future for you?

Change Agent

What is a change agent? A change agent is someone who understands the dynamic forces and factors that influence change. He or she understands the importance of change as a catalyst for growth and organizational vitality. Many church programs and structures are irrelevant. They are simply trapped so deep in the past that nothing short of radical change will bring them back to life. The most valuable leaders in the future will be those who know how to bring about organizational change. Leading the change in the African American church is going to be one of the most challenging tasks facing the preacher. This task is so important that I have dedicated all of Chapter Eight to the subject.

Christian Innovator

What is a Christian innovator? Pastors of the new millennium will need to be men and women who are creative thinkers or smart enough to surround themselves with creative people. All around us innovations in technology are changing the way we live and interact with each other. All of these new ideas are the results of people being innovative and creative.

An innovator is someone who is able to creatively develop new methods and strategies for doing ministry in today's turbulent world. He or she is someone who has the ability to generate more effective results from scarce resources. Innovation is experimenting with new ideas, seeking new ways of doing things, and allowing God to lead the congregation to continuous renewal and change. Innovation is moving beyond and ignoring the cries of "we have never done this before" and doing what is necessary to bring renewal and change to a church. Innovators will always have thriving and growing congregations.

Spiritual Enabler

What is a spiritual enabler? A spiritual enabler is someone who helps persons and churches discover the power of faith through a deeper commitment to God. Spirituality is the channel through which persons are brought into a deeper, more intimate relationship with God. When Moses was trying to lead the Israelites to Canaan, he tried to do it all by himself. His father-in-law, Jethro, told him that his primary responsibilities were to train the people to lead, walk upright before them, and be their spiritual guide and intercessor (see Exodus 18:19-20).

Those who are members of Generation X and the Baby Boom generation are in search of a deeper relationship with God. These are the generations of people who are intrigued by the spiritual but have very little interest in the church. The leader who is able to develop ministries that spiritually empower persons and bring them into a deeper relationship with God will lead a growing church. The next big population group is called

Generation Y. They are the 57 million youth under the age of 15, according to the Wall Street Journal.[2] Where are the young adults, those between the ages of 18-32? Are they present in your church?

Pastoral Authority

One of the biggest problems in many churches has to do with the question of authority. Bernice King, daughter of the late Dr. Martin Luther King, Jr., remarked, "In the past decade, there has been a move of God that is requiring our houses of worship to come in line with the Word of God and to reflect the power and authority of God--or else lose His favor."[3] The contemporary church lives in a world that has little regard or respect for authority. Shawchuck and Heuser point out that "since the 1960s, a pervasive mistrust of leaders has crept into the very fiber of the American ethos. A feeling pervades that our leaders are not to be trusted."[4] Many times these beliefs of rebellion and individualism are manifested in the church. The behavior of distrust might manifest itself in several ways. The pastor may be intentionally excluded from receiving information about the financial operation of the church. Decisions by the pastor may be overly scrutinized, overturned and even rejected. New ideas are placed in a death chamber of apathy and inaction. Pastors may be tolerated and not genuinely loved and respected by the lay leaders.

There have been occasions when lay leaders have given the impression that they must protect the church from the preacher/pastor. In some way or another, he or she is going to take advantage of the church and leave the congregation in disarray. That is why it is imperative that churches be guided by the Holy Spirit in the selection of its pastoral leader.

Ironically, there are many congregations which have reduced the pastoral office to one of being a hired hand--someone subject to the supervision of deacons, trustees, or some other power hungry individual(s). Clearly, those congregations are out of order. Simon Chan has noted what must be the believer's position regarding submission and obedience.

> The Protestant doctrine of the priesthood of all believers has sometimes been distorted into a me-and-my-God egocentrism. We think that because we have direct priestly access to God, we owe obedience to God and no one else. We forget that obedience to God may well come through freely embracing the yoke of human authority. The ancient monks taught us that learning to be under obedience to a human superior is one of the most effective ways of checking our self-will. And self-will, not ignorance, is what hinders us from perfect conformity to God's will.[5]

The people of God must develop a heart and mind that is willing to submit to the authority of God and His Word. I don't want to be one-sided in this matter of authority. It is crucial that pastors "walk their talk." The pastor must have the spiritual interest of the people first and not his own interest. I know of pastors who are more concerned about what they receive for their birthdays and anniversaries than they are the church's welfare. "Congregations expect competent church leaders, but they also want pastors who possess inner character and integrity--a congruency between what they profess and what they do. For a variety of reasons, the journey inward is resisted by many."[16]

We want to finally settle this question of authority once and for all. In this section, we are going to consider the authority of the pastoral office. We want to discuss the questions: Who holds the legitimate authority of church leadership? Is there such a thing as a democratic form of government in the church of Jesus Christ? What has happened to the biblical concept and teachings on the theocratic rule of God?

The word authority means that one has the right to govern or lead. Jackson Carroll states that "authority is legitimate power."[7] He further stated that "to have authority is to use power in ways that a congregation or other church body recognizes as legitimate, as consonant with and contributing to the basic beliefs and purposes of the church."[8] The legitimacy of the pastor's authority is grounded in who he/she represents. The pastor speaks for God, the Eternal One, who is Creator and Savior. Eddie Long wrote the following about pastoral authority:

> It doesn't come from my credentials, my training, or my personal accomplishments. My authority to say such things doesn't come from anything I have done or from any particular gift or ability that I possess. It comes from the Word of God and the destiny God

sovereignly ordained for us. I am one of God's many "scarred" leaders who were chosen for their brokenness and weaknesses instead of their strengths. My authority comes from God's inexplicable decision to send me to the church and the nation with a message.[9]

Biblical Definitions of Authority

One of the issues that confronted Jesus during His ministry was the question of authority. "And when He had come into the temple, the chief priests and the elders of the people came to Him as He was teaching, and said, 'By what authority are You doing these things, and who gave You this authority?'" (Matthew 21:23). There were many occasions during His ministry wherein Jesus had to defend and define the source of His authority. One day Jesus answered His critics saying, "And He gave Him authority to execute judgment because He is the Son of Many" (John 5:27). The authority of the preacher/pastor is given by the same One who received authority from the Father (see Luke 9:1-2). Jesus gave His disciples the authority to demonstrate power from God in their work. The church of Jesus Christ is a theocracy, that is, it is God-governed. God has appointed leaders to give direction to the work of ministry.

Leadership Nugget: **"In order to have the oneness of the Body, there must first be the life of the Head and then the authority of the Head. Without the life of the Head, there is no Body. Likewise, without the authority of the Head, there is no oneness in the Body."**

Watchman Nee

The word "authority" is translated in Greek by the word, *exousia.*

"The New Testament concept rests on three foundations. **First**, the power indicated is the power to decide. **Second**, this decision takes place in ordered relationships, all of which reflect God's lordship. **Third**, as a divinely given authority to act, exousia implies freedom for the community."[10]

Let's examine briefly the sources of pastoral authority. Where does the pastor's legitimate right to lead the congregation come from? Who gives the pastor the legitimate right to make pertinent decisions on behalf of and for the church? No human authority can make rules or laws that subjugate, denigrate nor otherwise delete, deflect or deny the pastor's office of its legitimate authority. We cannot legislate away the pastor's legitimate right to lead. When a church does that, it removes the spiritual authority for God to bring healing and wholeness to a congregation. Sometimes churches will remove the possibility of God doing miracles in the church because of their disrespect for the pastoral office. There is nothing in the church or outside of it that supersedes the Word of God, not constitutions nor any other man-made rules.

Pastoral authority is not invested to us by God to placate special interest groups. The pastor's authority must never be politicized. He or she must be free to lead and direct the activities of the congregation. God's authority is given to us to lead His people through the treacherous paths of life.

The Sources of Spiritual Authority

- The Word of God, Hebrews 13:17.
- The Call of God to ministry, Mark 1:20; Luke 5:1.
- Ordination to the gospel ministry, 1 Timothy 4:14.
- The authority of the pastor comes from the office he holds, 1 Timothy 3:1.
- Consecration by the Holy Spirit for the work of ministry, Acts 13:1.
- The commission of Jesus Christ to feed His sheep, John 21:15-17.
- Submission of the congregation to pastoral leadership, Hebrews 13:17.
- The spiritual nature of the church, 1 Peter 5:1-4.

The Sources of Organizational Authority

- Licensure by the local church.
- Call to serve as congregational leader by a local church.
- Church governing bylaws and constitutions.

One of the primary lessons we need to get from this chapter is the importance of recognizing the pastoral office as being ordained by God. Further, it is crucial to respect and allow the pastor to lead the congregation.

Duties of Key Leaders

"Deacons likewise must be men of dignity, not double-tongued, or addicted to much wine or fond of sordid gain ..."

1 Timothy 3:8

Throughout this book, we have been looking at leadership in the church. We have looked at the duties of leaders in general. Now we want to take a look at some specific leadership positions and their responsibilities to the church and pastor. We will begin with the deacons/deaconesses, followed by the trustees and other financial leaders in the church. We will not consider all of the various other leadership positions that are in the church. Each congregation should develop its own job descriptions based on its needs and polity.

The Ministry of the Deacon and Deaconess

The office of deacon is the second biblical office recognized in the Baptist Church.[1] Deacons and deaconesses are servant leaders in the local congregation. In the New Testament where deacons are mentioned, it is in connection with the shepherds of the flock or congregation (see Philippians 1:1; 1 Timothy 3:8-13).[2] In his letter to the congregation at Philippi, Paul recognized the two groups of leaders present in that church, overseers (bishops) and deacons. **"Paul and Timothy, bond-servants of Christ Jesus, to all the saints in Christ Jesus who are in Philippi, including the overseers and deacons" (Philippians 1:1).**

The office of church servant was first instituted by the apostles of the Jerusalem church, to meet a specific need that had developed within the congregation. **"Now at this time while the disciples were increasing *in number*, a complaint arose on the part of the Hellenistic *Jews* against the *native* Hebrews, because their widows were being overlooked in the daily serving *of food*" (Acts 6:1).** The apostles convened a meeting of the congregation to discuss and resolve the issues relating to the perceptions or problems involving favoritism being shown to the native Hebrew widows. **"And the twelve summoned the congregation of the disciples and said, 'It is not desirable for us to neglect the word of God in order to serve tables'" (Acts 6:2).**

Seven men were chosen who became the prototype of the deacon (see Acts 6:5). The men were chosen by the congregation based upon a set of spiritual qualifications. The final approval and appointment resided with the apostles. **"But select from among you, brethren, seven of good reputation, full of the Spirit and of wisdom, whom we may put in charge of this task" (Acts 6:3).**

The word "deacon" is from a Greek word **diakonos**, which means servant. There were two primary reasons that the position of deacon was created. The first was for the purpose of freeing the apostles to do the work of the shepherd of the flock, which included teaching, preaching and prayer. **"But we will devote ourselves to prayer, and to the ministry of the Word" (Acts 6:4).** The second reason was to make sure the widows of the congregation and those who were in need were given the proper care and attention they needed.[3] The deacons were selected and set aside or consecrated to serve tables. **"And these they brought before the apostles; and after praying, they laid their hands on them" (Acts 6:6).** The laying on of hands was an official form of public recognition of their selection to serve the tables of the widows.

Biblical Role of the New Testament Deacon

It is apparent that the deacons within the church at Jerusalem were given specific responsibilities and authority. They were responsible for the service of tables within the church. This means that they were required to receive benevolent contributions and to distribute as needed. Strauch has identified four primary duties of the Seven:

- ❑ to collect money and goods contributed to the needy (Acts 4:34,35, 37; 5:2);
- ❑ to distribute the money or goods to the needy (Acts 4:35);
- ❑ to ensure that the church justly and fairly distributed the money; and
- ❑ to coordinate the church's overall charitable services to the needy.[4]

Through the work of the deacons, the early church was able to provide consistent and constant care for its widows and most needy members. The seven were equally responsible for assisting the poor of the Christian community throughout Jerusalem (see Acts 2:44, 45; 4:32-37; 6:1).[5]

Common Misconceptions About the Role of Deacons

In many churches today, there is intense and unnecessary conflict over the role of the deacon's ministry. Unfortunately, many Baptist churches have adopted a practice that is not biblical, in any sense. We have called our deacon's ministry the "Official Board" of the church. The very language of "official board" is unbiblical and fosters the idea of a group that makes policy and determines the direction of the church's ministry. The erroneous notion of deacons/deaconesses as the official board has its genesis in the "Restoration Movement" that took place in the 1890's. No one really knows when the idea of "boards" found its way into the church. It appears from what I have discovered, the idea of "church board" began within the Disciples of Christ congregations and spread from there to other denominations. No one really knows how that movement took flight throughout the churches in America. Arthur Harrington has documented well the origin of this corporate language that found its way into the church of Jesus Christ.[6]

Perhaps the most unlikely creature to be evolved by the Restoration Movement in its developing concept of church leadership has been the Official Board of the church. In an endeavor committed to the restoration of the New Testament faith and practice, its development is a particular enigma. In fact, it has always proven to be something of a theological embarrassment to the movement; and since no Scriptural apology can be made for its existence, little has ever been written about it. In the first one hundred years of the weekly *Christian Standard*, so scarce was any reference to it that there is not even an entry or category for it in that Journal's index. Perhaps even more amazing is the fact that, in almost two hundred years, no one has ever addressed its origins. David I. McWhirter, the Director of the Library and Archives of the Disciples of Christ Historical Society in Nashville, probably the most complete collection of documents of the Restoration Movement, writes:

In checking our holdings I find that we have approximately ten books which talk about the Church Board. I am quite sure that none of these discuss the origin of the Church Board but simply tell how it should work. In talking over your topic here at the Society, several of us are in agreement that the Church Board probably developed rather gradually. There is probably no "first" Church Board as such.

Now isn't that remarkable? In a movement committed to restoring the church of the New Testament, something as big and important as the church board was allowed to develop and exist within the church with its origins going unquestioned and uninvestigated for all these years![7]

Richard L. Dresslhaus, an Assemblies of God pastor, has furthered this idea of deacons as an "official board" in his book, *The Deacon and His Ministry*. Baptist congregations are beginning to see the fallacy in this type of leadership structure and are moving away from it to a more biblical description of what deacons and deaconesses do in the church. Given all that has been stated, what are some of the misconceptions about the roles of deacons and deaconesses in the church today?

- ⊗ Deacons are overseers of the church.
- ⊗ Deacons are pastoral supervisors.
- ⊗ Deacons are the official board of the church.
- ⊗ Deacons are the final approving authority in the church.

All of the evidence suggests that the twenty-first century church will need to rethink these issues and questions if it is to make a difference in the future.

Role of the Deacon/Deaconess in the Church

The role of the deacon in the church has to come from the original intention of the Apostles who first established the office of church servants in the church at Jerusalem. What I say regarding the deacon applies equally to the deaconess. The New Testament does not specifically define the role or function of the deacon. Here are some broad guidelines that should be useful:

☞ Assist the pastor in the conduct of the church's mission.

☞ Care for the church membership.

☞ Look after the church's widows and orphans.

☞ Assist pastor in conflict resolution.

☞ Help congregation to support pastor's vision.

☞ Model spiritual conduct and behavior.

☞ Assist in the teaching ministry of the church.

☞ Provide spiritual leadership in the church's ministry.

☞ Assist in the care of the pastor and his family.

Qualifications for the Office of Deacon/Deaconess

The ministry of the deacons and deaconesses is very important in the local church. It should never be minimized nor taken lightly by the occupants of the office nor the congregation. The early church recognized the importance of the ministry and developed a list of strict qualifications. When these selection criteria are followed, they relieve the church of any and all struggles for power and domination among its key leadership core. The list of qualifications is found in 1 Timothy 3:1.

☩ Persons worthy of respect and dignity.

☩ Not double-tongued, "wishy-washy."

☩ Not an abuser of wine or strong drink (drugs).

☩ Not greedy for money or the control of money.

☩ Persons who practice sound, biblical doctrine.

☩ Family-oriented.

☩ Teachable.

☩ Servant-oriented.

☩ Spiritually motivated.

Responsibilities of the Servant Ministry Leaders

What are the responsibilities of servant ministry leaders? Detailed below is a list of responsibilities that are scripturally based, that servant leaders in the church should follow in fulfilling their ministries.

- The leader of the ministry of the deacons/deaconesses must take heed to his personal spiritual development and growth.

- The leader must resolve to submit to the authority of the Word of God.

- The leader must strive to follow and work under the authority of the pastor of the congregation.

- The leader should know and understand the mission of the church and the various ministries it is seeking to carry out.

- The leader, along with the pastor, is the primary teacher of the other members of the deacon's ministry.

- The leader should organize the deacons/deaconesses to fulfill the biblical and constitutional mandate of the congregation.

- The leader should ensure the pastor has the necessary time for study, prayer and meditation for teaching and preaching.

- The leader should seek to understand the needs of the pastor and his family.

- The leader should give biblically, and teach the members of the deacon's ministry to give according to the biblical patterns.

♦ The leader should meet with the pastor periodically, to prepare for church meetings and regular meetings of the deacon's ministry.

♦ The leader should periodically check to ensure that the deacons are following through with their individual ministry assignments.

♦ The leader should ensure that members are present for Weekly Prayer Meeting and that persons are assigned to lead the prayer and praise service.

♦ The leader should encourage other leaders in the church to attend and give support to the spiritual life of the church.

♦ The leader should seek to resolve all minor conflicts without involving the pastor. All major conflicts should be immediately brought to the pastor.

♦ The leader should ensure that the widows, the sick and those who are hurting are given the necessary spiritual support and comfort.

The Ministry of the Church Trustees

Under Virginia law, churches are prohibited from incorporating. Some state laws permit and/or even mandate that churches be incorporated. The laws vary from state to state, and it is best to check with the Secretary of State where you live, as to the specifics and laws that govern incorporation of local churches. The laws of Virginia provide for the establishment of a group of people who serve as representatives of the congregation in legal matters. The specific Virginia laws establishing the role of church or religious organization trustees are Code of Virginia 57-8, Code of Virginia 57-9, Code of Virginia 57-12, and Code of Virginia 8.01-220.1:1.

There is a false and misleading belief that church trustees can be held liable for church debts or obligations. The Code of Virginia is specific: Church trustees cannot be held individually liable for any of the church's debts or obligations, unless they exceed their own proper church authorization or engage in behavior and conduct that is willfully illegal or without church authorization. The requirement in some states is that at least three (3) persons be designated, by a church vote, to serve as legal representatives for the church. These three persons are, in turn, registered with the Circuit Court of the city or county in which the church is located. You should always check and see what the requirements are in your state or locality.

The trustees are the only persons authorized to convey church property, and sign for and encumber the church in debt, provided it is done with the proper church authorization. James Sheffield remarked: "The office of trustee is necessary because of the relationship of the church to the state. Because the trustees should only act at the direction of the church, they are considered as church officers rather than a committee."[8] The discussion about boards applies equally to church trustees. Trustees do not comprise a board! Boards, by definition, set policy and approve strategy for an organization. Trustees in the church serve as servants for the congregation's resources.

We live in a time when the American economy and society are very complex. Churches have more assets, both financial and physical, than they had in previous generations. It is crucial for church trustees to be better trained and attuned to changes in vital areas of physical plant and financial asset management.

Trustees are resource managers. They can serve many valuable functions within and for the local church. When trustees perform their jobs well, the local church is strengthened and provided with the resources it needs for effective ministry today. Congregations and denominational organizations will need to begin conducting better and more realistic training for church trustees. Below is a list of duties that are the minimum that church trustees are responsible for.

- Trustees serve as legal representatives of the church. They should make recommendations to the church regarding the retention of legal counsel in matters where counsel is needed. They are the official representatives of the church in all matters of litigation.

- Trustees hold the title and deed to all church property. This in no way gives trustees ownership or control of the church's property. They are responsible for safeguarding the legal documents that attest to church ownership of property and equipment.

- Trustees sign all legal documents relating to the purchase, sale, mortgaging, or rental of church property. Only those persons registered with the Clerk of the Circuit Court are required to sign, and then only with the vote and approval of the church, at a regularly scheduled or called business meeting.

- Trustees are responsible for maintaining the church's property, buildings, grounds and equipment in a state of proper repair. This includes every facet of physical plant management. They are charged with the securing of the necessary supplies and equipment to maintain the buildings and grounds. Trustees are responsible for the maintenance of all office equipment and furniture of the church.

- Trustees are responsible for conducting an annual inventory and survey of church property for damaged and/or missing items. They are responsible for conducting an annual fire and safety inspection of the buildings and grounds to ensure that a high state of safety exists. They should inspect all fire safety equipment and ensure that it is working. They should see to its proper use in an emergency.

- Trustees should periodically review and update all church insurance policies to include fidelity bonds.

- Trustees should be familiar with the local zoning codes that impact the church in the municipality where they reside. They should stay abreast of all property in the community for possible future purchase.

- Trustees should be knowledgeable of all the tax laws, state and federal, and how they impact the church. The trustees should be familiar with the reporting procedures, forms, dates, and deposit locations for all state and federal tax filings.

■ Trustees should be familiar with all Virginia and federal laws that relate to employee/employer relations.

■ Trustees should be familiar with the endowment program of the church and its long-term financial objectives and investment strategy. Therefore, trustees must be knowledgeable of financial markets and investment strategies to ensure the long-term financial viability of the church.

■ Trustees should be familiar with the church policy file and personnel policy.

■ The trustees must work in concert with the pastor, treasurer, deacons/deaconesses and financial secretary to ensure the proper management of all of the church property and assets.

■ The trustees are responsible for the proper disposal of all property to be discarded by the church.

The role of the church trustees is essential to the smooth and efficient operation of the church. The tasks assigned to them are not to be minimized.

The Role of the Trustee Ministry Leader

We have already seen that leadership is crucial for an organization. It is extremely critical that the leaders of the trustee ministry of the local church have a deep, abiding relationship with the Lord.

- He or she must take heed to their personal spiritual development through daily prayer, Bible reading and study, and Christian ministry.

- The trustee ministry leader ensures that the trustees serve the best interest of the congregation, follow the church bylaws, and allow the ministry to function under the leadership of the Holy Spirit.

- The trustee ministry leader works under the leadership of the pastor to ensure that the real and personal property, financial resources, and human resources of the church are properly cared for.

- The trustee ministry leader helps mentor and develop future trustee ministry workers and leaders along with the pastor.

- The trustee ministry leader seeks to promote the spiritual growth and mission involvement and support of the trustees.

● The trustee ministry leader ensures that the church has the resources necessary to carry out the mission mandate of the church.

● The trustee ministry leader works with the church treasurer and financial secretary to ensure that the church stays financially solvent.

The Ministry of the Church Treasurer

The ministry of the church treasurer is very important. The treasurer should be a person of high moral and spiritual character. They should be organized, patient and discreet. They must also recognize that God is the owner of all church funds. Listed below are several of the duties of the church's treasurer.

✓ The treasurer must take heed to his or her personal spiritual development and growth.

✓ The treasurer is the chief custodian of all church funds and bank accounts. He/She deposits all funds in church approved banks and institutions.

✓ The treasurer opens and closes accounts as the church deems necessary.

✓ The treasurer maintains an inventory of the safe deposit box.

✓ The treasurer leads an ad hoc committee on weekly church expenditures.

✓ The treasurer receives the weekly receipts from the counting committee, verifies the weekly deposit, deposits the receipts in the bank and maintains a record of all deposits made by the church.

✓ The treasurer ensures that all church checks and official records are maintained in a secure file at the church.

✓ The treasurer renders reports to the pastor, trustees, and church periodically as required or requested.

✓ The treasurer keeps a record of all receipts and expenditures.

✓ The treasurer is one of three persons authorized to sign checks drawn on church bank accounts.

The Ministry of the Financial Secretary

The financial secretary can be an officer of the church and/or a paid employee. The financial secretary should possess basic bookkeeping and accounting knowledge, or be willing to be trained. Further, the financial secretary should have demonstrated management and computer literacy skills. Because this is a position of trust, the same rule that applies to other spiritual leaders in the church must apply to the financial secretary. The financial secretary must be concerned at all times with personal spiritual development and growth. The work is a stewardship trust that requires faithfulness to God and the ministry of the church. The financial secretary must see himself or herself as part of a ministry team consisting of the pastor, treasurer, trustee leader and deacon leader. The financial secretary should never act independent of the financial leadership of the church. Listed below is a list of the tasks performed by the financial secretary.

- The financial secretary maintains all of the financial records, including all bank statements, bank accounts, investment accounts, scholarship funds, etc., for the church.

- The financial secretary records and maintains a record of the individual contributions of each member of the church.

- The financial secretary assigns each member a membership number.

- The financial secretary orders, inventories, and issues each member a set of envelopes for their giving.

- The financial secretary maintains a record of all the church's current, fixed and long-term (mortgages) debts.

- The financial secretary writes all approved checks, but should never, under any circumstances, be included as a signee.

✐ The financial secretary maintains on file a current balance sheet and income statement.

✐ The financial secretary prepares the monthly payroll for distribution to church employees.

✐ The financial secretary prepares all state and federal income tax reports, ensures that the proper amount is deposited in the bank when required, and prepares the necessary W-2 and W-4 forms.

✐ The financial secretary prepares quarterly and annual financial reports for distribution to the church membership.

Functions of Group Leaders: The Three Ministry Chairs

All church auxiliaries and committees have a formal organizational structure. The three primary leaders of church auxiliaries, ministries and committees are the president/chairperson, vice president/vice chairperson and the secretary. Each of these individuals has distinct functions within their organization. Every church leader should have a working knowledge of the church's governing documents, i.e., constitution and bylaws. Leaders should understand how decisions are made within the church and how to request operating funds. Group leaders should be knowledgeable of the major events and dates on the church's annual calendar and give their support to them. One of the most important skills that all group leaders need is meeting skills. They should have a working knowledge of Robert's Rules of Order. While the church does not operate by Robert's Rules, they are necessary when conducting business meetings.

Duties of the Ministry Team Leader

1. Serves as the auxiliary's spiritual leader.
2. Maintains Christian fellowship within the group.
3. Leads and conducts group business meetings.
4. Plans the meeting's agenda.
5. Leads group discussion during business meetings.
6. Leads in planning group activities and tasks.
7. Leads group training sessions.
8. Leads in developing group goals.
9. Delegates tasks to other group members.
10. Coordinates group activities with church calendar.
11. Motivates group members to achieve group goals.
12. Understands the needs of group members.
13. Appoints committees and assigns work tasks.
14. Serves as a member of the Pastor's Council.
15. Works with and for the pastor of the church.

Duties of the Assistant Ministry Team Leader

1. Serves as a spiritual leader.
2. Helps maintain Christian fellowship.
3. Assists the leader in leading the group.
4. Presides at meetings in the leader's absence.
5. Works with the leader in planning and coordinating group activities.

6. Assists in group training sessions.

7. Assists with group motivation.

8. Understands the needs of group members.

9. Works to foster the church's interests and goals.

10. Works with and for the leader of the group.

Duties of the Ministry Team Secretary

1. Serves as a spiritual leader.

2. Helps maintain Christian fellowship.

3. Records the minutes of all business meetings.

4. Prepares and reads the minutes of previous business meetings.

5. Maintains and preserves the group records for future use.

6. Corresponds with other churches through the church office.

7. Prepares a copy of the minutes prior to the meeting for the president's review, corrections and signature.

8. Contacts group members to pass along important information regarding the group.

9. Maintains a current file of group member's addresses and telephone numbers.

10. Works with and for the president of the group.

The Challenges Facing Black Church Leades

"For the time will come when they will not endure sound doctrine."

2 Timothy 4:3

The last decade of the twentieth century has seen some of the most dramatic changes in American Christianity. We have been privileged to witness the dawning of a new era in Protestant Christianity in America and all around the world. There have been many major changes that have had a decided impact upon the African American Christian church. Let me assert further here that the face of the African American Baptist church is in the midst of undergoing a very radical change. We are in the midst of a twentieth century religious revolution that will leave many of our churches floundering in the dust of their own apathy and/or inability to change. This will, in turn, lead many churches into a period of tremendous stagnation and eventual death. We are not just seeing a shift in the religious paradigm, rather, we are seeing new paradigms being developed each day by religious and spiritual visionaries who do not necessarily embrace our traditional Baptist way of doing things. And, even among our ranks, there are new paradigms being created which are altering the way that our children and grandchildren see and understand church.

Many of us talk about changing the traditional Baptist church into a new model of spiritual power. Yet the truth is we have very little understanding as to what a traditional Black Baptist church looks like, let alone how to lead it to change.

As we look toward this millennium, a great deal of emphasis is being placed on preparing the church for the future. I want to suggest that we are already living in the new millennium, which technically begins with 2001. The church of the Lord Jesus Christ will face challenges unlike any that she has faced in the history of the modern world and even the history of human civilization. Indeed the Black Baptist church in America is already reeling from a host of internal and external forces that are wreaking havoc on our traditional membership base. One of the realities we face is the slow, steady decline of traditional Black Baptist churches. In many rural communities, churches are not growing. Some have not taken in a new convert in years. Many of us believe that our churches will go on forever. This is not true. And leaders deceive themselves if they believe that God will allow churches to continue if they do not address serious needs among their members and the fallacies of their structure and programs. We need to begin to address this issue of declining congregations.

As we think about the challenges we face as contemporary Black church leaders, one of the questions we want to raise is, What are the factors or forces that will impact the church's efforts or attempts to become the spiritual and loving community of faith? The pressures that we will encounter will come from within and without. Within we will face the challenges of dealing with a new generation of Christians who have been nurtured differently than their parents and grandparents. Further, we will face the ominous task of leading change in congregations that are bent on staying the same. Outside of the lofty confines of our bastions of spiritual power, there is a growing tide of people who see the church as being out of step with the times. They believe that the church offers nothing of real value to life, particularly in this high-tech age. Outside of the walls of the church, we are dealing with a cultural revolution that wants to be spiritual but not Christian nor members of a local church. This will and is already having a significant impact upon the church and how it is viewed today. Another question that we must ask is this: What are the perceptions that men and women have of organized religion today? I hope to begin to open the door for dialogue in this chapter. It is my desire to flush out some thoughts and reflections that have been a part of my own pilgrimage as a denominational and church leader in a radically changing religious and social environment.

Leadership Nugget: **Begin to see your challenges as opportunities to become creative and innovative. Identify your main problems, then seek spiritual guidance on how to address each of them.**

Shifting Trends and New Paradigms

Paradigm has become a very popular word in the church and business communities. In his book, *Paradigms: The Business of*

Discovering the Future, Joel Arthur Barker gave this definition of a paradigm: "A paradigm is a set of rules and regulations (written or unwritten) that does two things: (1) it establishes or defines boundaries; and (2) it tells you how to behave inside the boundaries in order to be successful."[1]

Think of a paradigm this way. At the beginning of the twentieth century, the American economy was driven by the massive development of industry. America was the world leader in manufactured goods. A man or woman did not have to possess a great deal of intellectual skill in order to earn a high salary. Today the American economy has shifted from manufacturing to information technology. Therefore, it is increasingly important that those who wish to maintain a middle class lifestyle will need to develop new skills in information technology. There has been a paradigm shift in America. Things have changed. The rules of survival in the workplace have changed.

The world is changing so rapidly that keeping up is almost impossible. The rules have changed. We have witnessed in our generation, under the leadership of a democratic president, the beginning of the dismantling of the American system of social welfare. Who would have ever thought that such a thing would have happened? Corporate downsizing, the Internet, the World Wide Web, e-mail, global economies, and disinflation are all part of the landscape of American culture. The rules have changed.

Corporations and organizations that recognize and adjust to the paradigm shifts will continue to be successful. The ones that do not recognize these shifts and fail to make significant organizational and programmatic changes, will not be successful. They will continue to have difficulty competing. The competition is everywhere. It is worldwide! Burt Nanus has pointed out that healthy organizations expect and embrace change as a key to survival and success.[2]

The Black Church Facing New Paradigms

The most important question facing leaders of our denomination today is this: What are the factors that will determine our long term success or failure as a denomination? Further, what are the things that the national convention needs to be engaged in that will strengthen the state conventions, which in turn can strengthen the local churches? What are the kinds of skills our leaders need to have today? What do we need to do today to prepare leaders for tomorrow?

One of the things that we will have to face is the cost of integration on our traditional membership base. When you look at religious programming on television, just look at the number of Black faces you see in non-Black churches. Who would have ever thought that you would see Black faces sitting behind Charles Stanley at the First Baptist Church in Atlanta? I am in no way holding up a flag and saying that this should not be. What I am asserting is this: Black churches will have to become more aggressive and assertive in their evangelistic efforts. We must face the fact as pastors and church leaders that people have choices and they do not have to belong to or attend our churches. There are far too many other viable options that individuals can give their time and money to. One of the most interesting phenomenons is the number of Blacks who attend and are members of predominantly White congregations. There are predominantly White mega churches that have more Black members than many local Black churches.

Thirty Trends Impacting Black Church Life

Understanding trends and their impact upon our culture is crucial to developing ministries that are both relevant and effective. *Webster's New World Dictionary* defines a trend as "to extend, turn, incline, bend, etc., in a specific direction; tend to run." The idea is that a trend is something that moves in a specific direction toward something. Trends are not the same as "fads." A fad is a temporary phenomenon. For example, when I was a young man, I wore bell bottom pants and platform shoes. It was the "style." A few months later the style had changed and if I was going to keep up, I would need to change my wardrobe. Trends are not temporary. They tell us that a permanent change is coming. They let us know that whatever the style was, things are about to permanently change. Trends are patterns of social behavior that impact the way people live. Trends tell that a paradigm shift is about to take place. Leaders should be on the lookout for new trends; they will have a decided impact upon your ministry. Joel Barker has suggested that trends do not take us by surprise; they have a history. They leave a clear path from which we can forecast their direction.[3] They gather momentum slowly. He stated further that "even if we do not like the shape and content of the emerging trends, they at least give information that allows us to anticipate certain consequences."[4] What follows are thirty trends that I believe have had a significant impact upon the African American church and community. How we address them is for each church and its leaders to decide.

1. Suburbanization movement from the inner city to suburbs
2. Greater affluence among Black Americans
3. Increase in the number of Black college graduates
4. Spread of AIDS among Black men and women
5. Increase in the number of single parent families
6. Widening of the gender gap between Black men and Black women
7. Increase in the number of youth having never attended church
8. Widening economic gap between rich and poor
9. Welfare reform
10. Increase in the number of Black women entering prison
11. Increase in the number of Blacks who are members of non-denominational churches
12. Increase in the number of young Black men attending church for the first time and being baptized
13. Increase in the number of Black women entering seminary and full/part time ministry
14. Rise and spread of new religious movements among Blacks, i.e., Full Gospel Baptist Church and independent churches
15. Shift toward more charismatic worship among Black churches
16. Rise of the Black mega churches in large and mid-size metropolitan areas

17. Reverse migration from the North to the South
18. Continuing rise and spread of Islam among Black males
19. Aging Black church leadership, both clergy and lay persons, and the absence of young church leaders
20. Shifts from religious liberalism to spiritual conservatism, which is evidenced in the changing nature of politics in America from liberalism to conservatism
21. Greater thirst for Bible knowledge among baby boomers
22. Changing values and morals among Black churches
23. Absence of the use and presence of information technology in the majority of Black churches
24. Shift from traditional church membership to non-traditional membership patterns
25. Television and proliferation of television ministries and churches
26. Dwindling financial resources for the church, in a rising tide of economic affluence and expansion
27. Greater mobility through improved transportation
28. Spread of state lotteries and legalized gambling
29. Acceptance of mainstream contemporary Gospel Music and the shift toward more contemporary church music
30. Absence of young adults in the church, especially males

Challenges to the Creation of Christian Community

What are the obstacles that you will face in your efforts to create a spiritual, Christian community? Each of these obstacles represent a challenge for the leaders of the church. Let me share briefly some of the challenges that will have a decided impact upon the social and communal life of the local church.

First, we face the assimilation and inclusion of people who have never been a member of a Christian church. What happens to the communal life of a traditional Black Baptist church when people who have never been affiliated with a local congregation join? How do we develop meaningful relationships with people who are coming to the church to seek a greater spiritual connection? What happens when new members encounter traditional bureaucratic snarls that tie the church down? What happens when we receive affluent, sophisticated, and educated new members who really want to make a difference in the lives of others, only to be denied? In the Jerusalem church they experienced that exact phenomenon when the Holy Spirit convicted and convinced more than three thousand souls. One of the tasks of becoming the beloved community is to become the community before we invest a great deal of effort in evangelism and church growth. We may not be prepared to receive a great influx of new members. These are questions that each individual congregation has to address. Denominations can give some guidance and offer some training, but the church has to be open to new faces.

Second, we must reach a generation of unchurched Black males and young men with the message of hope and encouragement. C. Eric Lincoln and Lawrence Mamiya, in their study of Black church life, report that this is especially critical in the Northeast and Western urban centers.[5] In their study of life in urban areas, they cite work done by Dr. Ruth Dennis of the Meherry Medical School which states that while we see evidence of individuals returning to church, there is also "evidence of the church . . . losing ground as it relates to Black male youth, adolescent, young adult and adult."[6] Black males face some of the most blatant and overt racism in America today. A 1996 report published by the W. K. Kellogg Foundation pointed out the dilemma that Black males face in America today.

> The African-American male holds a peculiar, uncertain status in American society. In some realms of life, such as athletics and entertainment, he is a highly respected, often revered figure. More generally, however, the African-American male is too often labeled as the epitome of all that is violent and criminal in our society.[7]

The problem that we face in evangelizing our own people is that when and if we bring these young men into the church, they encounter a culture that is so radically different from what they know from the inner city street life or even in the prison of jails, that they leave without being connected to the church.

Third, we must counter the myths and over exaggeration of prosperity and high living, which is a natural by-product of faith in the God of the Bible. I believe that God does create wealth and give us the power to get wealth (Deuteronomy 8:8-17; 28:1-13; 1 Chronicles 29:13.). However, today there is a whole new generation of tele-evangelists who espouse a theology of prosperity that undermines fundamental Christian stewardship. Therefore, new believers may be disappointed by the failure of a local church to teach, preach and produce the step-by-step plan that will produce the kind of wealth they are looking for.

Fourth, we must recognize that we live in a time when the social norms have changed, and therefore the church must work extremely hard to create and foster the Christian community. There is an entirely different social morality at work in the world today. People have no problem defending and promoting social co-habitation as an acceptable lifestyle. There have been a few individual congregations that have given consent to the whole notion of same sex marriages and relationships. It is nothing for young couples to live together today, then come to the church and seek the blessing upon their union without ever moving out prior to their wedding. All of these changes in social morality place pastors under a great deal of pressure, many times, to accept and affirm what he or she knows to be biblically wrong. In many instances there is a clear attempt to negate the authority of Scripture for our own authority. However, it is only as we allow the preacher to be true to the biblical teachings, that we see the creation of a community that is socially and morally pure. Even in the New Testament churches there were instances of believers falling into sexual sin and immorality (see 1 Corinthians 5:1; 10:8-9; 4:17-19; Galatians 5:19-20).

Fifth, we face the task of creating ministries that reach children and youth with the gospel. Youth ministry is no longer an option for the church, it is a must. God commanded that the Israelites would teach their children their faith and share their story of deliverance (see Deuteronomy 6:4-6; Joshua 4:1-7). Planning youth ministries today is far more challenging and necessary than it was twenty, even ten years ago. How will we reach young people with the gospel?

Sixth, leaders face the task of developing ministries and means for helping believers develop spiritually. The church is a spiritual organism. People today are seeking deeper spiritual experiences. Dynamic worship is only one aspect of our modern day spirituality. There must be some way of returning to the "Desert Fathers" and renewing some of what they have taught us about spiritual formation. Churches are simply full of people who gather weekly, sing a few songs, hear a prayer, listen to a sermon, and then return to their empty worlds. How do you help believers to develop spiritually?

Strategies for Addressing Some of the Challenges

The church will need to understand the forces that are at work in the world today. Church leaders will need to have one eye on the sky and another on the ground to hear the coming roar of the next new trend. I have listed what I believe to be some of the strategies or suggestions that we must employ as African American Christians today.

1. We must become courageous enough to confront a cynical society with the message that the gospel is the good news about Jesus Christ. We must develop ministries that take seriously the task of evangelism. Establish schools of witnessing in the church.

2. Increase the commitment level of "professing believers" in the validity of the gospel's claims and support for the mission of the local church. Teach and preach on the

claims of the kingdom upon the lives of God's people. Create a deeper sense of God's call, and deepen the importance of God's purpose for the church.

3.   Overcome institutional stagnation that breeds religious and spiritual apathy by leading the leaders into a season of spiritual renewal and revival. Help the church to see the biblical picture of the New Testament church.

4.   Create a climate where the past can be celebrated, the future embraced, and change accepted. Never discard the experiences of people because you want to do something different.

5.   Discover new ways to empower lay members and lay leaders to become more responsible for the growth of the church and the expansion of its ministry. Help believers discover their spiritual gifts, equip them for service and release them to do ministry.

6.   Foster a climate of Christian community and fellowship where believers can grow spiritually, intellectually, and experientially. Lead the leaders in the church in a study of relational leadership and how to become more compassionate and sensitive.

7.   Invite a new generation of African American young adults and youth to embrace our historical faith and to

appreciate its significance for our heritage. This will involve the creation of new ministries in the church. It would be insightful to solicit ideas and thoughts from young adults as to why they are not active in the church.

8.   Re-focusing our vision so that it becomes Christo-centric. The church has become too focused on its social agenda in some cases. In others we are politically oriented. Lead a period of rediscovery of the life and teachings of Jesus Christ. Have a period wherein members can reaffirm their commitment to Jesus Christ and the kingdom work.

Change:
The Key of Church Visions
8

"And no man puts new wine into old wineskins, else the new wine will burst the old wineskins, and the wine is spilled, and the wineskins will be marred; but new wine must be put into new wineskins."

Mark 2:21-22

In the summer of 1997, Rosetta and I, along with another pastor and his family, went to London, England. One of the things that I wanted to do while in England, was see some of the great churches where men such as Charles Haddon Spurgeon and D. Martyn Lloyd-Jones had stood. I was not prepared for what we ran into. London, like many European cities, has lost contact with the Christian faith. There were very few people who could tell you where there was an active and viable congregation worshiping. We attended a midweek worship service at a church in York, England, and it was filled with pomp, circumstance and boredom. On the Sunday that we were in London, Rosetta and I went to Brixton, a Black neighborhood in London. There we found several different congregations that were alive and filled with enthusiasm. These congregations appeared to be growing and were very vibrant, unlike the rest of the churches we saw in London, York, and Paris. Several of the congregations were led by pastors who had come from Africa. These churches manifested great spiritual fervor and fire in worship. They were, obviously, going to be the spiritual future of London and England. The church of England, to me, did not appear to have much life. The churches were more for museum tours than worship centers. Even Westminster Abbey is noted for its beauty and for who is buried there, which may explain why it is dead for worship. In Europe, the church did not change and Christianity has nearly died. The same could happen here without real, relevant change in the church.

Initiating and implementing change in the traditional Black Baptist church, or any church for that matter, is one of the greatest challenges facing the twenty-first century pastor or church leader. Getting people to accept change and new ideas has been compared to trying to teach elephants to dance. If there is one thing that kills a church's vision, it is the thought that it may lead to change in the congregation. Later in the chapter, I will discuss why there is resistance to change in congregations.

Let me assert further here that the face of the African American Baptist church is undergoing a very radical change. Many of the traditional models we have used for programs and organizational structure are not having the same impact that they once had. Traditional Baptist churches are still using organizational models that were created forty or fifty years ago. New times demand new structures. New models for ministries and structures will need to be developed. As we look out over the horizon of this new millennium, a great deal of emphasis is going to be placed on preparing the church for the future.

George McCalep stated that the inability of the church to change is probably one of the most prevalent factors limiting church growth.[1] The loss of credibility from national religious leaders, lack of meaningful programs, and the emergence of new splinter groups that have drawn away congregations are also major factors that inhibit church growth. Many of the problems with slow growth, and in some cases no growth, are products of our own making. We saw the wind of change shifting in another direction but simply failed to follow it.

Leadership Nugget: **The key to leading change in the church is in being focused, flexible, Christ-centered, Spirit-led and spiritually empowered. Without these qualities, your personal strength will be insufficient for the journey.**

The Struggle to Change

Change is the one great nemesis of progress and growth in the church. It is the intense struggle to initiate and maintain change in the church that wears out many leaders in traditional churches. There may be as many reasons why people resist change as are our efforts to introduce it. Many African American churches tend to be very slow and resistant to change and progress. This is not just true of African American churches, but it is generally true of congregations, period. Someone has said that the last words of the church were: "We have never done it this way before." Shawchuck and Heuser state that "change has the ability to thrust even the strongest organizations into decline. The decline is not due to change but to the organization's response to it."[2]

We live at a time in which new changes take place before we can absorb the previous ones. Who would have thought ten years ago that the Internet would generate tens of billions of dollars in economic growth in this county. Fifteen years ago, e-mail was not a common household word. I had never heard of e-mail fifteen years ago. In fact, I didn't even own a personal computer until 1990. When we brought our first personal computer in 1987, there was no one on the church staff who even understood how to use one. In fact, I had never used one and did not even know how to turn it on. There are still churches today that do not own a computer nor do they see the value of having an Internet connection. How can the church be effective in its ministry, when it refuses to do the things that are necessary to be technologically up-to-date? We live in changing times in a changing world. One of the tasks of leadership in this new millennium will be leading change in the church. The local congregations will have to change if they are going to succeed in their mission. Shawchuck and Heuser remarked how changes in the religious climate in America have impacted the church.

Changes in American society regarding faith, spirituality, worship preferences, feelings about religious institutions, and so on, over the past three decades, have proven a bane for many churches. At the same time, however, these changes have proven a blessing for the so-called mega churches, the large pastoral churches and the great number of congregations who have freely, quickly, and effectively responded to the changes in American religious preferences.[3]

The interesting thing about the change in American religious preferences and interests is that they are not surprises. The new face of religion did not sneak up on us. We saw it coming every time we turned on the television and watched religious programming. What is tragic is that we failed to respond to the new waves washing up on the shores of the beach. Many of us saw them as fads and did not realize that they were trends that were here to stay. My wife reminds me that there may be pastors and church leaders that don't know what to do about change. They may want to change, but they don't know where to start or how to initiate change in their churches. Later in the chapter I offer some suggestions for getting started with change in the church.

Change in Traditional Black Baptist Churches

Many of us talk about changing traditional Baptist churches into new models of spiritual power. I write about traditional Black Baptist churches, not to be exclusive, but it is what I know and it is the context of my own ministry. The principles that are stated here can be applied in ministry context. Changing a traditional Black Baptist church has led to nightmare experiences for some pastors I know. They felt as though they were under siege because of their efforts at trying to get the church to change.

Remember, these churches can be changed as well. Remember, the key is timing and strategy.

What are traditions and why do they cause so many problems in churches today? Tradition is one of those subjects that people have different ways of thinking about. We don't all agree as to what tradition is and how it is to be observed. I am not against tradition. No! I am for tradition. I believe that we must observe those traditions that have their roots in Scripture. Tradition is very important in the Bible. God wanted Israel to observe annually their deliverance from Egypt through the celebration of the Passover (see Exodus 12:23-27). The church remembers the birth, death and resurrection of Jesus through the traditional celebrations of Christmas, Good Friday, and Easter. These are very important traditions in the church. However, some of the things that have been established as traditions may in fact keep some congregations from becoming more relevant and effective.

In this section, I believe it is important to understand how tradition is being used and defined. There are probably several definitions of tradition. Aubrey Malphurs stated that churches interpret the Bible differently based upon their divergent traditions, and this produces various church traditions. He wrote:

> I define church traditions as the nonbiblical customs, practices, and ideas that church people attempt to observe and pass on to the next generation. They serve to preserve the past. These traditions include such practices as a Wednesday night prayer meeting, singing

the great hymns of the faith, maintaining a Sunday School program, the way in which a church takes the offering and so forth. Traditions are nonbiblical because Scripture doesn't mandate them. The church observes these practices in such a way that in time they become an integral part of the congregation's overall identity and ministry. Because the church so highly values these customs, they attempt to preserve and pass them on to the next generation.[4]

Notice several key elements in this definition. Church traditions are customs that have developed within the congregation over a period of time. Second, they have no basis in Scripture. Third, church traditions are things that one generation seeks to pass on to the next generation, thereby institutionalizing the traditions. These activities or events can be passed on and become ingrained traditionalism. Jim Petersen defined traditionalism this way: "Traditionalism is the excessive respect for tradition that gives it the status of divine revelation."[5] If we examine many of the traditions that exist in our churches today, we would discover that they have no basis in Scripture. Many traditional churches are having a difficult time fostering and maintaining growth. People today want to be a part of a dynamic spiritual experience that brings them closer to God and gives them a great cause they can commit their lives to serve. Let's take a few moments and take a look at a typical, traditional Black Baptist church.

Twenty Characteristics of A Traditional Black Baptist Church

1. They are organized around departments and boards, deacons, deaconess, trustees, and a joint board.
2. Trustees count and control the money.
3. There are multiple choirs, and there is often conflict in the music department.
4. The church calendar drives the church year and not the needs of the congregation. Anniversaries and special days are held as the primary fundraisers.
5. Sunday Schools may or may not be a separate organization in the church.
6. The music is Euro-centric and is driven by something other than the people's likes.
7. There is slow growth, usually less than ten percent of the active membership of the church.
8. The number of older members outnumber the younger, newer members.
9. The pastor is not the real leader of the congregation. His or her authority is restricted by lay leaders who want and seek control of the church.
10. Attempts to change the status quo are soundly defeated.
11. There is an absence of committed disciples and workers for ministry.
12. Worship is usually at 11:00 A.M., Sunday School is at 9:30 A.M. and Wednesday Night Prayer Meeting is at 7:30 P.M.
13. The members know very little Baptist doctrine or polity.
14. There is very little training and spiritual development.
15. Drums are not present in the church.

16. There is an absence of contemporary art forms, i.e., praise dances, step teams, drill teams, and rites of passage programs.
17. New members are not fully assimilated into the church.
18. Positions of power are reserved for a select few of the congregation.
19. Major decisions are politicized out of existence.
20. Decisions are often entangled in bureaucratic snarls.

Congregations may exhibit some or all of these traits. A church would have to exhibit more than seventy-five percent of these to not be considered a traditional church. Let me clarify here that I am not announcing a death sentence for traditional Black Baptist churches. These congregations have been instrumental in producing many great church leaders. However, this is a new day and it will require a rethinking of what it means to be the church in this millennium.

The Role of Spiritual Leaders in Leading Change

It is obvious that if the church is going to make an impact upon the secular world that we live in, churches are going to have to change. Change will have to be an organizational endeavor that includes every leader in the church and not just the pastor. That our congregation needed to change became increasingly clear to me as I sought to lead our congregation to fulfill its ministry and mission. Second Calvary is a traditional congregation with a great history. The church was organized in 1879 by men and women who were former slaves.

It became obvious to me after seeing our growth plateau and strong members leaving the church for other congregations, that we needed to move in a different direction. There was something about what we were doing that was not quite effective. Our greatest year of growth was in 1992 when we received 167 new members. After that, we began to see small decreases--149 in 1993, 141 in 1994, and down to less than 100 new members by 1999. In addition, we were seeing people come and go. I asked the Lord to show me what to do. The Lord made it plain to me that Second Calvary would have to change if we were going to go to the next level of ministry. Change had to begin in my heart and spirit before it could and would take place in the church.

Pastoral leaders are going to have to become bold and coura- geous in this new millennium. Too many pastoral leaders are afraid of the people and lay leaders in the church. Why is this so? They have been victims of abuse, many times by lay leaders who are sworn preacher antagonists. Their calling, as they see it, is to protect the church from any fly-by-night schemes of the pastor. Because we have politicized the church of Christ, we have taken away the leader's ability to lead with vision and courage. God does not want us to be afraid of their faces (see Jeremiah 1:3-11). According to Shawchuck and Heuser, "The only congregations that will thrive in the coming decades will be those whose leaders have learned to respond to change, not resist or ignore it."[6] Leaders are going to be the catalyst for change in the future. Leaders will be challenged to give birth to new ideas and challenging the people of God to take risks and try something different. Some churches are going to resist change with every ounce of their strength.

The Role of Leaders in Change

What ought to be the leader's role in helping to give birth to change in the church? **First**, it is important for pastoral and key leaders to assess their own spiritual growth and feelings about the current state of the church. He or she must lead the spiritual leaders in the church to examine the church's ministry and effectiveness. One of the first keys to leading change is time in personal study, prayer, and reflection about the church and contemporary movements in church growth. Only then can they assess the internal climate of the congregation. Is there real numerical and spiritual growth in the church?

Second, leaders must seek the heart and will of God for the congregation. The pastor must begin to ask God to give him or her a fresh vision for the church, and share that with the other leaders in the congregation. I think it would be helpful to bring the leaders of the congregation together, just for prayer and praise. Building their spiritual life is crucial to whatever the church is going to do. Prayer is the most effective means for creating a climate of spiritual unity among the leaders in the church.

Third, leaders should study the methods and means used by churches that are growing to determine what they are doing right. I am not advocating that a church copy another church's program or ministries. Ministries are contextual, and they do not transfer from one church to another. Upon assessing what growing churches are doing, it is important to grasp the principles that led to their growth and not try to use their methods. Many times pastors don't want to ask pastors of growing churches what their strategies were. As Baptists, we must break out of the mold that only other Baptists can help us. There is only one church, and whatever you learn from ministries that are effective and growing is going to be helpful in your church's ministry.

Fourth, pastoral leaders will need to teach the congregation the biblical doctrine of the church. Only when the congregation understands its biblical and spiritual nature and purpose can change begin to take place in the church. Many churches are more culturally defined than they are biblically defined. In many instances we have been so busy being Baptists that we have failed to be biblical. Don't get me wrong, I am in no way declaring that you should abandon your denominational roots, whatever they are. Just don't allow that to keep you from discovering what the Scriptures teach about the church and its purpose.

Overcoming Resistance to Change

We tend to accept change in every segment of life but are very slow to see the benefits of change as a catalyst for church growth and progress. Leaders in the church will have to become competent in leading change in the church. William Bridges has pointed out that changes do not create the problems, it is the transitional process that usually creates the conflict and ultimately kills the new idea.[7] Change is situational. The new program, the new ministry, and the new policy all lead to change.[8] These are all situational. Transition is the internal and mental processes that people go through when trying to come to terms with the change.[9] If we can effectively manage the mental and psychological processes, and minimize conflict, change can take place in a smoother manner. Notice, I am not saying that you will not experience some opposition, you will. Just expect it and don't be surprised by it.

How to Overcome Resistance to Change

- Be clear in your mind first as to exactly where God is leading you.
- Be open to the people about God's vision and what it may require.
- Be prepared for resistance.
- Be open with your leaders and share your vision with them.
- Be committed to training the leaders and church about the future.
- Be clear about what the New Testament teaches about the church.
- Be prayerful, spiritual, and open to the leadership of the Holy Spirit.

Why People Resist Change

Why do people resist change? Leaders have to understand that there is never just one reason why people are resistant to change. There may be several different reasons from different groups of people in the church who are opposed to a given change. Many times it may depend on whose area of ministry, power, or influence is being threatened. I listed some reasons why people resist change below.

- ⊗ Change is a threat to our sense of security.
- ⊗ Change means altering the traditional way things have been done.
- ⊗ Change means venturing into uncharted territory.
- ⊗ Change represents a loss of control.
- ⊗ Change means the loss of the "authorship" of new ideas.
- ⊗ Change means a loss of identity.
- ⊗ Change means shifting power and influence to new people.
- ⊗ Change means letting God decide what He wants for the church.

Key Elements in the Change Process

1. **Managing change**

   The key is managing the process in such a way as to minimize confusion. Management is the process of getting things done through people.

2. **Effectiveness**

   The idea of effectiveness has to do with the impact or difference that is made. The object of change management is to do it in such a way as to have a positive impact upon the church and leaders.

3. **Processes**

   Process is concerned with how we move from point A to point B with a minimal amount of resistance.

Factors that Can Lead to Organizational Change

What are the factors that lead to organizational change in the church? Is it important to know what can produce change in a church? Knowing what can lead to organizational change helps us better prepare for it.

- **Change in organizational leadership**
    - a. New pastor
    - b. New chairperson
    - c. New ministry team leader
- **Change in the church's circumstances**
    - a. Internal/External
    - b. Economic, i.e., welfare reform
    - c. Political
    - d. Social
- **Growth of the leader**
    - a. Leaders grow over time
    - b. Leaders grow through attendance to workshops
    - c. Leaders grow through personal study
    - d. Leaders grow through spiritual pilgrimages
- **Growth of the church**
    - a. Numerically
    - b. Spiritually
    - c. Carnally
    - d. Economically
    - e. Educationally
- **Emerging Trends**
    - a. National
    - b. Economic

    c. Religious

    d. Local

- **Crisis**

    a. Conflict within the church

    b. Leadership crisis

    c. Community crisis

- **New Vision for the future**

    a. God's call for spiritual renewal in the church

    b. Decline that leads the church to believe the only alternative is renewal

Why Change is Important

☺ Allows the church to stay fresh and focused.

☺ Means that the church recognizes that growth is not static.

☺ Allows the church to adjust to new circumstances.

☺ Creates a climate wherein visionary leadership can be followed.

☺ Keeps the church attuned to the progressive revelation of God.

☺ Enables the church to capitalize on emerging trends and new directions.

☺ Keeps the organization from becoming institutionalized and stuck in its own traditions.

☺ Makes room for new leadership gifts and talent

Steps in Implementing Change

○ Recognize and celebrate the past.

○ Discuss the proposed new changes with deacons and trustees.

O Discuss the proposed new changes with key leaders for input and ratification.

O Disseminate information among the congregation on proposed new ideas and changes.

O Allow for discussion, disagreement, negotiation, reconciliation and ratification.

O Adopt the proposed changes for implementation. Continue to review the proposals for adjustment.

Leader Responsibilities in Change

● Thoroughly understand the proposed changes.

● Communicate accurate information when questioned.

● Be open and honest about concerns, feelings and apprehensions about the proposed changes.

● Never communicate negative feelings you may have about the proposed changes. The Lord may convert you to see the benefit of the changes to the church.

● Support the pastor's vision and reasons for the change and its long-term benefit to the church.

● Always recognize the church covenant and its teaching of the right of the majority to govern.

The one key element of change is maximum participation in the process. The more participation and the greater the communication, the more likely the implementation of the change.

Vision and Courage: The Key to Leading Change

"The Lord answered me and said, 'Record the vision and inscribe it on tablets, that the one who reads it may run. For the vision is yet for the appointed time ...'"

Habakkuk 2:2-3

Effective, spiritually anointed Christian leaders of the future will be men and women with the courage to take risks and seize fresh opportunities to make an impact for the kingdom of God. They will be men and women with vision, who are able to bring about change, develop new church structures, and meet the challenges of twenty-first century ministry. I include courage along with vision because I believe it takes courage to stand up for a vision that God has given to you, especially at a time when people want to minimize pastoral leadership.

The Importance of Courage

Courage is one of the most indispensable traits that a spiritual leader can cultivate. Why? Because the very work of the kingdom is at stake. If the leader is afraid, the followers will loose heart as well. In the Old Testament, a sterling example of courageous leadership can be found in Joshua and Caleb.

During the time that Israel was traveling through the wilderness, Moses was commanded by God to send twelve spies to search out the land of Canaan and bring back a report about it (see Numbers 13:1). When the spies returned, ten brought back a negative report, saying that they were not able to go into the land that God had already given them. The people in the land were giants, and they (Israel) were no more than grasshoppers in their sight (see Numbers 13:25-29, 31-33).

Joshua and Caleb brought back a "minority report" saying that the land was fair and that because God had already given it to them, they were able to conquer and subdue it. They had the courage to stand up to ten of the senior tribal elders and leaders in the nation. Joshua and Caleb were more concerned that God's will be done, as opposed to looking at the size of the opposition. When Joshua became Moses' successor, God told him to be courageous and that He would be with him (Joshua 1:1-9).

Spiritual leaders look at tough situations and devise plans and strategies to overcome the obstacle based upon God's will and purposes. If the church is to succeed in a culture that's growing more secular day by day, it must be under the spiritual leadership of individuals who are more concerned that God's will be done than they are about their personal safety and well-being (see Acts 4:17-21).

There is no one, living or dead, who exemplified more courage than Jesus Christ. He came to earth knowing the outcome of the journey (see 2 Corinthians 8:9). He came knowing full well that He would be nailed to a Roman cross, crucified, and buried in Joseph's tomb. Paul stated that God has highly exalted Him and given Him a name that is above everyone's name (see Philippians 2:5).

What is courage? Courage is Harriet Tubman continuing to lead slaves to freedom in spite of the constant threat to her life. Courage is Nat Turner's willingness to die first, rather than remain a slave. Courage is Frederick Douglas overcoming the denial of an education by his slave master, only to become one of the most eloquent men to have ever lived. Courage is Jackie Robinson breaking the color line in baseball even though whites did not believe a Black man was equal with them on the field. Courage is Muhammad Ali risking his heavyweight title of the world, to maintain his manly dignity. Courage is Martin Luther King, Jr. going to Memphis, TN, even though he knew that his life had been threatened. Courage is my mother and father accepting a call to a congregation that had seven living members and was housed in a storefront building. What more shall I say; do we need any more examples of courage?

Leadership Nugget: "Oppressed people cannot remain oppressed forever. The yearning for freedom eventually manifests itself, and that is what has happened to the American Negro. Something has reminded him of his birthright of freedom, and something has reminded him that it can be gained."

Martin Luther King, Jr.,
Letter From Birmingham Jail

There is no substitute for courage in the heart of the leader. His or her courage is contagious and can infect the hearts of his or her followers. The courage of the leader in the face of death defying odds can create a burning spirit for victory in the hearts of your followers. When I was an army officer, it was important to never convey a spirit of fear or intimidation when faced with difficult situations. Without the courage to see through the vision that God has put within your heart, you are not likely to succeed.

The Importance of Vision

Vision is one of the great buzz words of the twenty-first century. We hear a lot of talk about vision today. Everyone has one or is looking for a vision. Vision is crucial for the success of a church's ministry. Vision is where you see God taking your ministry. Vision is the "new thing" God is going to do through your ministry. It is what God shows you that your church's ministry can become. Vision is seeing something that you have never seen before, particularly as it relates to the ministry of the church. Without vision, you are not going to get very far. Let's consider several definitions of vision.

Burt Nanus: Vision is a realistic, credible, attractive future for your organization. It is your articulation of a destination toward which your organization should aim, a future that in important ways is better, more successful, or more desirable for your organization that is the present. Vision is where tomorrow begins, for it expresses what you and others who share the vision will be working hard to create.[1]

Robert Cueni: Vision addresses the possibilities for congregational mission and ministry by offering a positive way to talk about the past and present. It also images what might be in such a specific, attainable way that change can be perceived as a worthwhile possibility. Most important, congregational vision must be more than reasonable and socially relevant. It must be theologically sound.[2]

Aubrey Malphurs: Vision is a clear and challenging picture of the future of a ministry as you believe that it can and must be.[3]

Great movements are begun with a vision and achieved with daring and courage. Satan dares us to take a stand for God and then commit ourselves to that stand. He dares us to be concerned about the least, last, lost, and the left out in our communities. With God's vision we can address the issues and questions related to poverty, injustice, racism, educational failure and economic disparities in our society.

The writer of Proverbs 29:18a stated, "Where there is no vision, the people perish." Great congregations are congregations that have great visions. Strong ministries are ministries that have vivid imaginations and plenty of creative energy. Robert K. Greenleaf wrote, "Not much happens without a dream. And for something great to happen, there must be a great dream."[4] George Barna stated that "vision for ministry is a clear mental image of a preferable future imparted by God to His chosen servants and is based upon an accurate understanding of God, self, and circumstances."[5] Barna has given what he believes are the key components of vision. I want to list them here.

KEY COMPONENTS OF VISION

* **A Clear Mental Image**

    A vision is a mental picture of what you would like to see happen in the future. It is a picture of things and conditions that do not currently exist.

* **Preferable Change**

    Vision is never about keeping things as they currently are; it is always about change. The focus of vision is always on what is preferable in improving the ministry and future of the church.

* **A Future Focus**

    Vision is never a focus on yesterday. Vision is always about tomorrow. The vision should challenge the congregation to think outside of the box and see possibilities that they have never seen before. It concentrates on the future, rather than trying to replicate the past. It is a deliberate approach at influencing the future direction of the church. Vision proclaims that God wants us to move in a new direction, one that we have never been before.

* **Imparted By God**

   Vision is a reflection of what God wants to accomplish through the church and you, to build the kingdom. If the vision is not given by God, it will not succeed. His anointing must be upon the vision. Hence, it is concerned with the mission and purpose of the church in the community.

* **A Chosen Leader**

   Leadership is the most important element in realizing the vision of God for the church. Only a leader can galvanize the resources and people together for positive action and re-direction of effort and energy.

* **Understanding God**

   Leaders must have an understanding of God that is grounded in Scripture. We must be able to comprehend His will for the church's mission and ministry. God is the sole object of our affections and worship.

* **Know Yourself**

   In developing a vision, one must know oneself, one's abilities, spiritual gifts, limitations, values, and desires. Vision is never an attempt to promote self, your dreams or your ambitions. It is always the promotion of what God intends to do with and through His chosen people, the church.

* **Understand Your Circumstances**

Vision is never wishful thinking that is not grounded in reality. You must understand your situation in its entirety. The external and internal environmental factors will all play a part in developing a realistic vision for the future. Many churches have a Rip Van Winkle mentality. They went to sleep 50 years ago and have yet to wake up to the new realities of the twenty-first century. The Black church is facing tremendous pressure for the souls of its members. We must be real with what is going on around us and with us. You must know your community, your congregation and your competition.[6]

Steps in Implementing God's Vision

1. Pray for vision and direction for the church. God will give vision.

2. Conduct a Bible study on the church and its mission.

3. Prepare the church for the future by preparing them for change.

4. Appoint a vision community to pray with you and help

shape the vision of the future. Ensure that they are aware of their specific purpose and responsibilities. It is helpful to give them a vision and mission statement to guide their work.

5. Provide time and resources for the community to do its work. The vision community will need to become a learning fellowship. Shaping a new vision for the congregation will not only require prayer, but also, prayer and a clear discernment of God's will for the congregation.

6. Present the findings to the church, on a periodic basis, to ensure adequate communication of the vision. The more you talk to the congregation, thus including them in the process, the more likely you are to have success.

7. Allow adequate time for the work of the vision community to be discussed among the members of the congregation.

8. Adopt and implement the new changes incrementally. This allows time for evaluation and fine-tuning.

The Task of the Vision Community
1. Understand its purpose and mandate.
2. Train the committee in long-range planning.
3. Write a church mission statement.

4. Develop a list of strengths and weaknesses of the current ministry of the church.

5. Conduct a study of the community and its needs.

6. Conduct a study of the church and its needs.

7. Set goals for growing the church.

8. Select and develop long range action plans.

9. Communicate the plan to the entire congregation.

10. Implement and follow through on the plan.

Motivation: The Key to Organizational Success **10**

> *"I press on toward the goal for the prize of the upward call of God in Christ Jesus."*
>
> Philippians 3:14

One of the central tasks of leaders is keeping his/her followers motivated. The goal of every leader is to build a climate in which motivation can take place and be sustained.[1] Leaders are visionaries, enablers, equippers, planners, organizers, and motivators. It is important for those of us who lead to understand that we cannot motivate other people. Motivation is something that comes from within, it is a product of the individual's will and not the leader's. The leader can only provide the arena for positive motivation to take place. I believe that one of the most important skills for spiritual leaders in the church of Jesus Christ to learn is the art of motivation. We must be able to motivate ourselves and those whom we lead.

Leadership Nugget: **The most successful people are not the ones with the greatest talent or ability, but those with the highest level of motivation.**

Biblical example: Moses

Factors that Produce Motivation

There are three factors that I believe help determine our level of motivation. **First**, we are motivated by the **social environment** in which we live. A healthy social environment can create a positive environment for motivation to occur. **Second**, we are motivated by our **internal belief system**. The Apostle Paul believed that with God's help, he could do anything God willed in his life. The level to which we commit ourselves to our beliefs is a key factor to determining motivation. **Third**, our level of motivation is determined by our **needs**. Needs are important and drive everything we do, or fail to do, in life. We will say more about needs later.

Leadership Nugget:	**"The greatest talent of all is the ability to get others to use their talents fully."** **Dale Carnegie** **Biblical example: Nehemiah**

Hindrances to Motivation

As leaders, we are constantly having to deal with the same types of problems Moses dealt with in the wilderness. Complaints, murmuring, bickering, lapses in faith, and our people's grasshopper mentalities are common in many churches (see Numbers 14, especially verses 31-33). Many times people will come up with reasons why the church cannot do something rather than seeing the new possibilities created by God. A leader has to initiate progress and change by inspiring others to reach toward the goal.

William H. Cook in his book, *Success, Motivation and the Scriptures*, has developed a list of success stoppers.[2]

- If I only had more time to read my Bible....
- If I only had more power....
- If my work didn't make me so tired....
- If they would only ask me to do something....
- If I only had more talent....
- If God would just show me a sign....
- If my husband (wife) loved the Lord more....
- If I only had his/her education....
- If I only had more faith....
- If I could forgive myself....
- If our church wasn't like it is....
- If I had not made that wrong move....
- If they bragged on me like they brag on him....
- If I just knew what to say....
- If they ever elect me as a deacon....
- If my boss didn't have it in for Christians....
- If I could speak like the preacher speaks....
- If God didn't have it in for me....
- If I didn't have to live with my past....
- If my parents could just understand me....
- If only I could have lived when Jesus lived....
- If I didn't have to go to work so early....

The one common point in each of these statements is that we blame others for our personal failures. Leaders in the church tend to blame each other for programmatic failures. It is easy to

blame someone else for our failures, our mistakes, or our unwill-
ingness to work hard for success (see Genesis 3:8-13). Even great
men and women of God are not exempt from this sense of
defeatism and lack of motivation.

♦ Moses felt crushed and asked God to take his life,
    Numbers 11:14-15.
♦ Elijah wanted to sit under a juniper tree and die, 1 Kings 19:4.
♦ John the Baptist questioned the messianic claims of
    Jesus, Matthew 10:1-6.
♦ Paul was pressed in his spirit, Acts 18:5.

Oftentimes the many attacks of Satan, the struggles, the
challenges, the failures, and the disappointments associated with
ministry, can leave us frustrated and ready to quit. In the next
section, we will look at some principles that we can apply to our
situations to motivate those whom we lead.

Principles of Motivation

A principle is a law or rule that is always true, regardless of
the context in which it exists. There are several principles of
motivation that can be helpful to us in our efforts at motivating
the people we lead. Reginald M. McDonough has identified six
principles of motivation.[3]

Principle Number One

**A person's motivation is the product of their will.
Internal and external factors impact motivation.**

Remember, you and I cannot motivate anyone. They must do it themselves. The leader has to create the climate and conditions for motivation to exist. We can do that by creating a climate of support and love. Leaders offer incentives and seek the things which encourage a person to motivate themselves. Leaders must understand what is going on around them and with the people they are leading.

Principle Number Two

People are motivated by the desire to satisfy their basic needs for self actualization and fulfillment.

God has created us in such a way that we are at our best when we achieve our personal goals and desires. We are need-driven, whether positive or negative. We have primary needs and secondary needs. Primary needs are what we need in order to survive--food, water, shelter, air, etc.[4] Secondary needs are our social needs, our relational needs, and our need to be in fellowship with others. When our most basic needs are met, we are then motivated to meet other needs.

Principle Number Three

Human behavior is seldom the response of a single need. We may be responding to a variety of needs.

Humans are very complex beings. Human behavior is equally complex and sometimes difficult to understand. Our behavior may be motivated by a combination of things and not a single need. We eat to satisfy a basic physiological need for food, yet we can also eat as a result of feelings of rejection and low self-esteem.[5] Persons may need their name called in church not because they want to be seen, but because as a child they were always put down or were never praised as someone who made a significant contribution. Many people in congregations suffer from low self-esteem and need to be encouraged. A leader can never assume that people are driven by what we perceive to be their motivations.

Principle Number Four

Needs are satisfied in the order of their importance.

Leaders must be aware and sensitive to the fact that at different points in the lives of their followers, different levels of needs are operating. There are needs that are common to all of us because we are human. Then there are needs that we seek to fulfill or satisfy because other levels of needs have been satisfied. Social scientists have tried to identify various levels of needs in our lives. One of the hierarchies of needs was developed by Abraham Maslow. We are going to look at his hierarchy of needs.

Abraham Maslow's Hierarchy of Needs

Level Five	Self-Actualization
Level Four	Self-Esteem
Level Three	Belonging
Level Two	Security
Level One	Physiological

At the lowest level is the need for human survival. At this level we are more concerned about food, water, shelter, and the basics of life. The second level deals with our need for safety and freedom from fear. We have a need to feel free from the threat of death or bodily harm. The third level deals with our need to be in communities and fellowship with other human beings. We need companionship and friendship with others. The fourth level deals with our need to feel good about ourselves and our achievements. Everyone wants to feel special in some way or another. The highest level is our need to reach our fullest potential. The U.S. Army has a slogan--"Be All You Can Be." Humans have a fundamental drive and need to be all they can. All humans want to feel that they have accomplished all that they can in life. This is the level of meaning and purposefulness in living.

Leaders have to be aware that people whom they lead are operating along this scale of needs. There will be people in the group who are at one level or another at any given point. Therefore, leaders need to develop the ability to be tuned into where their people are.

Principle Number Five

As lower needs are satisfied, higher needs become more dominant in our behavior patterns.

One of the fundamental rules of successful marketing is knowing what motivates a customer to buy a certain product. When the marketer can identify and appeal to the motives of the customer, he/she can persuade the customer to buy their product. The same principle works in motivation. When one level of need has been met, the leader needs to recognize it. Once the need to belong to the usher's ministry has been satisfied, there may be a need to achieve a position of leadership or responsibility in the usher's ministry. Leaders need to be sensitive to individual needs to grow in ministry responsibility.

Principle Number Six

Growth-oriented motivation is superior to a deficit-oriented process of motivation.

Leaders are responsible for developing new leaders. As leaders, we must recognize that people have growth needs. Growth needs are needs that center on reaching the highest level of effectiveness in our ministries. Growing and nurturing disciples is a chief responsibility of the pastor/teacher and spiritual leaders of the church (see Ephesians 4:11-16). Granted there will always be people in the church who have no desire to change nor grow, but the majority of our people want to grow in their relationship with Jesus Christ and in their ministry. The leader has to recognize this fact and create the opportunity for personal spiritual growth.

The Growth Process

Need →→→ Goal →→→ Behavior →→→ Objective

The growth process is a continuous line that shows how we grow. Growth begins with a need.[6] Once the need is identified, we set a goal to achieve that need. Behavior is the result of our actions to achieve the final objective. Our goal as leaders is to enable and help believers grow in their relationship with Jesus Christ. The goal is sanctification.

Motivational Lessons Taught By Jesus

- ◆ Jesus understood the importance of purpose, Luke 4:18-19, 43.
- ◆ Jesus encouraged others to keep trying even after failure, Luke 5:4-7.
- ◆ Jesus knew the value of leadership training, Mark 10:35-45.
- ◆ Jesus modeled servant leadership, John 13:1-5.
- ◆ Jesus valued people, Matthew 4:23-25.
- ◆ Jesus included others in His work, Luke 10:1.
- ◆ Jesus was always straightforward with people, Luke 9:57-62.

- ♦ Jesus practiced and taught spiritual discipline, Luke 11:1.
- ♦ Jesus shared special moments with his followers, Luke 22:15.
- ♦ Jesus never shared His personal fears and doubts publicly, Luke 22:39.

Leadership Nugget: **Jesus Christ is the best model for church leaders to follow when it comes to understanding how to motivate God's people.**

Remember, one of the most important functions of leaders is motivating followers. We motivate by being able to exert a positive influence upon followers and the organization. Motivation is one of the primary means for increasing organizational effectiveness. This means that the leader has to seek to understand and apply the principles of motivation in his or her work with the people of God.

Jesus was the Master motivator during His earthly ministry. He was able to lead people to commit themselves to His purpose, even if it meant their death (see Mark 8:34). From the life and ministry of Jesus, we can learn many valuable lessons that will help us to become spiritual motivators. Nehemiah was able to motivate God's people to undertake a task that no one wanted and that had already failed once. Leaders are people who see success where others only see failure.

Building A Climate For Motivation

☞ **Be motivated yourself before attempting to motivate others.**

The leader of the group must demonstrate motivation before he/she can motivate others. If you are not motivated in your ministry, those whom you seek to lead will not be motivated either. They will soon become discouraged and give up. Nehemiah displayed courage in the face of opposition (Nehemiah 6:9-11). He was deliberate (Nehemiah 2:12). He raised morale and hope in the lives of his people (8:10). Have a positive attitude about your work.

☞ **Be sensitive to the needs of your people.**

One of the most valuable assets your group has are its people. Therefore, you need to know where people are in their lives and what they are dealing with. It is helpful to understand them and their needs. Create an atmosphere of trust and confidence by getting to know them personally. Be open to their pain and joy.

☞ **Create teamwork.**

A good team wins because the team members pull together. Stronger members are encouraged to make up for the lack of ability of the weaker members (see Luke 22:32; Galatians 6:2). Help others to see your vision by constantly communicating and sharing.

☞ **Always be positive when you refer to your group.**
Encourage mutual respect and cooperation among the group and within the church. Emphasize trust by giving

and showing trust. Create a climate where genuine love can exist (see Romans 12:9-10; Ephesians 4:32). Model love and respect in the group. Create a climate of team success by lifting up the abilities of each individual member. Never see God's work as impossible or improbable.

☞ **Affirm good work and achievement.**

One of the most effective ways to motivate people is through public recognition of their contributions.[7] Recognition is also one of the least expensive means to affirm good work and support. You can publicly affirm good work, write letters, and/or send small notes of appreciation and thanks. God affirms good work, and God's Word encourages us to affirm each other's achievements as well (see Matthew 25:14-23; Hebrews 6:10). Affirmation and recognition are essential in motivating others to work harder for the group.

☞ **Learn to share responsibility and authority.**

Incorporate new blood into the decision-making process. Many times good talent is always wasted doing busy work in the church. When you give a responsibility, give the authority to complete the task (see Luke 10:19). Authority gives the person the right to make decisions. Without the ability to make decisions, there can be no real growth in the organization. The growth of your various ministries are linked to the growth of the people who make up those ministries.

☞ **Keep the Christian challenge and mission in front of the people.**

Christian leaders must always remember that God has called us to mission and ministry. Our mission (Matthew 28:18-20) grows out of our commitment to God, which is the "Great Commandment" (Matthew 22:34-40).

☞ **Make organizational or group training a priority.**

Developing your group's ministry has to be a major priority. One of the reasons why some ministries suffer is because members do not feel that they are growing either in their relationship with God or in the ministry. Training increases skills and ultimately helps the groups standards of performance. Training can come in a variety of forms. Learning and development must become a priority with you. The group will function better when properly trained for the tasks. Peter Senge remarked, "The organizations that will truly excel in the future will be the organizations that discover how to tap people's commitment and capacity to learn at all levels in an organization."[8]

God has placed within each of us the desire and need to succeed at what we do. One of the primary tactics of Satan is to stifle our progress by planting seeds of doubt and apprehension in our minds. He is our adversary. However, with Jesus Christ as our guide and model, we can overcome any obstacle that gets in our way. When we are changed, our whole life is changed, including our minds and thoughts. Motivation is not something you do to others, rather it is the result of the positive environment that you create. Paul reminds us in Galatians 6:9, "And let us not grow weary in well doing; for in due season, we shall reap if we faint not."

The Purpose of Leadership Training

"All Scripture is inspired by God and profitable for teaching, for reproof, for correction, for training in righteousness; that the man of God may be adequate, equipped for every good work."

2 Timothy 3:16-17

Developing a continuous program to recruit and train leaders is one of the most important things a church can do. Leadership training is one of the best methods available for achieving church organizational goals. Reginald M. McDonough has pointed out that "without trained leaders, an endeavor has two strikes against it before it starts. The quality of work that a person can do is directly linked to his preparation for the task."[1] The Christian church has long held that learning and training were vital to ministry success and effectiveness. The early church, particularly the church in Jerusalem, was characterized by its commitment to study and learning. In recent years, we have not seen the same type of commitment to learning among pastors and lay leaders. Without trained leadership, it will be difficult for organizations to be successful. John Maxwell stated that the people closest to the leader will determine the level of success or failure of that leader.[2] Trained leadership will ensure that the organization has a pool of competent workers for ministry. Training improves organizational efficiency, leader competency and ministry effectiveness. Training church leaders works! The effectiveness of the church's ministry will depend, in large measure, on the effectiveness of the church's small group or auxiliary leaders. If they are untrained, unskilled, unspiritual, and nominal in their commitment to Christ and the church, they will create groups and followers who will mirror them. The church can go no farther than its leadership can carry it. Leadership training must become a priority and lifelong process for the church. The goal of every church should be to become a learning congregation. Thomas R. Hawkins stated this insight about learning congregations:

Congregations sometimes treat people as a utilitarian resource. Church members' time and abilities exist to help the congregation grow, develop more impressive ministries, or offer a wider range of programs and services. Learning congregations invert this formula. The primary shift in a learning congregation is from using people to create a better congregation to using the congregation to nurture better people. Experiences in ministry become occasions for reflection and learning, for constructing a fresh vision of new life in Christ. These visions then guide new acts of ministry and service in Christ's name.[3]

Training will need to be viewed as one of the keys to developing stronger, more spiritual congregations in this new millennium. No other area will be more critical than the area of leadership training. Leadership training has definite benefits for the church and the pastor. I believe that the cause of a lot of pastoral frustration is due in large measure to his or her inability to accept their role as a trainer and equipper of leaders. "Leadership is a group process. Leaders of large groups usually lead a small group of leaders who lead other small groups. Leadership is therefore the leading of a small group or the leading of a small network of groups."[4] When the pastor empowers others to lead, he is freed from many of the mundane tasks that go with leading the people of God to achieve the purposes of God in the world (see Exodus 18:17-23; Acts 6:2-3). Pastoral leadership and congregational leadership, at any level, is too demanding to be a one person show.

Leadership Nugget: **"Organizations learn only through individuals who learn. Individual learning does not guarantee organizational learning. But without it no organizational learning occurs."[5]**

Benefits of Leadership Training

In January 1984, I began an annual leadership training institute at Second Calvary. The purpose of the institute was to provide leadership training for newly elected and current leaders of the church. The James R. Jones Leadership Training Institute, as it is now known, has been one of the most effective teaching and transformational agents in our church. Second Calvary has benefited in countless ways from the sixteen years that the institute has been in existence. Some of the training benefits are listed below in what are key reasons why leadership training should be a part of every church's teaching ministry.

> **Training strengthens and unifies the church around a common center.**

Believers who are properly trained are likely to be more committed to the congregation's long-term and short-term goals. They see themselves as having a personal stake in what the church is seeking to do in the world and its community. Trained leaders understand that Jesus Christ is the center of the church's life, mission, fellowship, worship, witness, and ministry. They know that the real power in the church is not human, but spiritual.

When leaders are spiritually centered, those whom they lead will receive spiritually centered leadership. They will have leaders who know that God's will must be first and foremost in all things. Spiritually centered leadership blesses the church and God's people.

> **Training prepares believers for assuming leadership in the church.**

Church leadership is different from leadership in any other context. The church is concerned with matters of eternal significance. In the church we are training and nurturing believers to be Christian leaders, who mirror and model Jesus Christ. Training prepares believers for servant leadership responsibility. Further, the very nature of the organizational demands of today's church means that leaders must possess a different type of spirit, skill level, and knowledge. The church is the people of God who have been called to declare the gospel of salvation through Jesus Christ (1 Corinthians 1:2). The purpose of the church is different. The people of the church are different (see 1 Peter 2:9-10). These differences point to the need for a different type of leader.

> **Training equips believers for Christian service in and out of the church.**

The church is called to serve as God's agents of change in the world. Since the mission of the church is unique from any other enterprise, it is crucial that leaders understand that they are servants of dynamic spiritual and social change in and outside of the church. God calls each believer to some form of ministry, whether it be as a preacher, teacher, missionary, helper, encourager, prophet, administrator, deacon/deaconess, trustee, evangelist, youth worker, etc. As workers are equipped for service, the church is empowered to do more community outreach and missions.

> **Training equips believers for the work of evangelism and ministry.**

The single aim of the Christian church is to make disciples of men and women (see Matthew 28:18-20). God has called the church to be in partnership with Him through Jesus Christ (see 1 Corinthians 3:6-11). When we are properly trained in the purpose of evangelistic outreach and the most effective methods to use, our churches will experience continuous and steady growth (see Acts 2:41-47).

Most evangelistic efforts result in failure in African American churches because of two primary reasons. The first has to do with untrained witnesses for Christ who have no idea what to say or do when they confront unbelievers. The second reason grows out of the first. It is a lack of confidence in telling our story of salvation to strangers and acquaintances. Training enables us to confront our fears of witnessing and overcome them.

> **Training equips believers for everyday living.**

One of the most important things that Jesus did for the disciples was equip them for their new life in the kingdom of God. He taught them everything they needed in order to succeed in their work. His teachings, particularly the Sermon on the Mount, were filled with many practical lessons that enabled and enriched their everyday life.

Small group leaders are the first line of instruction for new converts in Christian discipleship. These are the people who are most likely to encounter new converts after the completion of an initial orientation period. Further, they are the most likely instructors for continuous teaching of new members about a local church, its policies and programs. Hence, they bear the unusual responsibility of helping to teach believers how to live for Christ.

One of the qualifications that Paul listed for the office of bishop in 1 Timothy 3:2 was the ability to teach others. A leader has to be able to teach the fundamentals of the Christian faith to others, while at the same time serving as a real life role model. We must recognize that even after people make Jesus Christ Lord, there are still other things that are high on their list of priorities.

Training enables believers to realign their priorities with God. Spiritual reinforcement and training is essential in small groups in the church. Training reinforces Christian teachings, beliefs and practices. The Christian life has to be practiced daily. When we are trained in the principles of Christian discipleship, we make stronger servants of Christ.

> **Training helps believers identify and use their individual spiritual gifts.**

According to the New Testament, each member of the body of Christ has received a spiritual gift. Paul likened the church to a human body with the various members having different bodily functions (see Romans 12:3; 1 Corinthians 12:4; Ephesians 4:7). Spiritual gifts are those special endowments of the Holy Spirit given to every believer for the purpose of building up the church and its ministry (see 1 Corinthians 12:7). George McCalep remarked that this is a major paradigm shift for many churches because they have been pastor-centered.[6]   Accordingly, spiritual gifts are given for the mutual benefit of the entire body.

Training enables believers to become knowledgeable not only of our faith, mission, ministry and message, but of our resources as well (see 2 Corinthians 4:7; 10:4). Training enables believers to appreciate the gifts of leadership given to the body of Christ (see Ephesians 4:11).   Further, training will enable believers to see the purpose of leadership within the body of Christ. Spiritual leadership exists to provide direction, inspiration, and to empower believers for the greater works of kingdom building.

> **Training distributes the church's workload among many members.**

The more believers are trained to do ministry, the more they understand the operational dimension of the church, the more they are able to participate in the life and ministry of the church. By training a variety of leaders for a variety of functions, the workload can be distributed among many more members. In Exodus 18:13, Moses tried to do all of the work by himself. This created a hardship for him and the people. When others are trained, it facilitates a fair and equitable distribution of the workload. In this way, a few people do not have to carry the bulk of the load while other members are mere spectators, which is so often the case.

The task of leadership is to involve as many people as possible in the work of ministry. When believers see themselves as needed, they tend to participate better.

Training equips others to teach.

The church is in constant need of spirit-filled, able, knowledgeable teachers of the Bible. Since the Bible is the chief source book of the church for all matters of belief, practice, conduct, and discipline, leaders need to be able to teach it effectively. As the church trains leaders and members in other vital areas of church life, ministry, missions, youth work, leadership, and witnessing, they develop skills that can be passed on to others.

The growth of the Christian church was fueled by teachers who passed on to others what they had received. In the New Testament church, teaching was at the center of its life (see Acts 2:42; 5:42; 11:26; 1 Corinthians 15:1).

Teaching is at the heart of the mission of the church today. The presence of so many different voices and influences necessitates that the church take seriously its mandate to teach (see Matthew 28:19-20). This means that those who teach must themselves be taught how to teach others effectively. Teaching for the sake of teaching is a waste of time. Those who teach are the cornerstone of the internal ministry of the church.

Training increases support for the church, ministry, and pastor.

The most important asset of any church is its membership support base. Trained members make stronger disciples and more committed supporters. The better trained and discipled the members, the easier the task of leadership. Untrained members tend to be rebellious and difficult to lead. People who have been properly discipled are an asset to the ministry. They tend to be more generous givers to the church and its ministry. They have a higher level of understanding regarding the work of the church and the various tasks and obligations that the pastor must constantly fulfill. The more leaders are trained, the more likely they are to understand the vision and direction of the pastor.

> **Training provides a forum for introducing new ideas and change to the church's leadership.**

Lyle Schaller has written that the number one issue facing churches, denominations, para-church organizations, seminaries, and other organizations is change.[7] Change is the most intense, divisive, heartbreaking, and difficult task for any leader to achieve.

One of the ways to introduce the idea of change within a local congregation is in the context of training. A training format allows for the introduction of new ideas and innovations in ministry. Training provides a forum for dialogue about new ideas and their impact upon the congregation. When leaders are involved in training, innovative and progressive ideas can be discussed and debated in a non-threatening environment. This enables pastors to determine the level of support or opposition to the new proposal. It also provides a way for group thinking to occur. In my book, there is no greater means for achieving growth and change in a congregation.

Training should never be viewed as a waste of time or money. Many times our expectations regarding attendance and participation by elected leaders may not match the results. A great deal of time and work may be spent planning and organizing the training event, only to have it poorly attended. Those responsible for leadership training must not be overcome by discouragement and despair.

The process of recruiting and training leaders in a local church is continuous. Because it is continuous, Christian educators and pastors should never lose hope. It is the long-term result of our efforts that we are more concerned about. The long-term spiritual viability of any congregation is determined by its present and future leadership. Preparation for the future begins now and continues into the future.

THE ROLE OF THE PASTOR

I have met and know too many pastors who have the misguided idea that leadership is total and absolute control of everything in, around, and above the church. They have a real need to feel in control, hence, they galvanize all of the authority and responsibility for every decision around themselves. The danger in this is that you will wear yourself out, and the members will become dependent upon you for everything. The role of the pastor is to develop and nurture other leaders who can and will lead others in the congregation.

In the process of developing leaders, there are specific tasks that the pastor is best suited for. They are listed below:

① Develop and refine his or her individual leadership skills.

② Sensitize the congregation to the need for new leaders.

③ Appoint a director of church training or leadership training.

④ Provide specific calendar dates for leadership training.

⑤ See that resources are appropriated for leadership training.

⑥ Develop innovative methods for leadership training.

⑦ Promote leadership training among the church's leadership.

⑧ Consent to serve as a teacher in the leadership program.

⑨ Bring in leadership specialists to lead retreats and conferences.

The Role of the Christian Education Ministry

① Study the leadership needs of the congregation.

② Support the work of the church training director.

③ Review and recommend curriculum materials.

④ Provide qualified instructors for teaching.

⑤ Determine and provide the necessary space for training.

⑥ Assist the pastor in developing a leadership training curriculum.

⑦ Develop programs to train youth leaders.

⑧ Ensure that equipment and resources are available.

⑨ Plan, promote, and polish the leadership training program.

The Role of Small Group Leaders

⇨ Recognize their need for on-going Christian leadership training.

⇨ Support and participate in church leadership training events.

⇨ Encourage their followers to participate in leadership training.

⇨ Study and read about Christian leadership.

⇨ Attend regional, association, state, and national conferences, workshops, and congresses.

⇨ Be supportive of the leaders of the church's leadership training program.

⇨ Implement the things that are taught and learned in leadership training.

⇨ Incorporate leadership training in their meetings.

⇨ Assist group members in discovering their spiritual gifts.

⇨ Encourage group members to use their spiritual gifts by creating opportunities for service.

⇨ Be open to change and new ideas.

Types of Leadership Training

Leadership training can be a very rewarding program for a local congregation and individual believers. "Individuals may identify new gifts or areas of service; skills may be sharpened for growth; and experiences may be shared that will instruct and inspire others."[8] Leadership in the contemporary church has to be broad and comprehensive. It must go beyond the traditional Bible Study, Sunday School Teachers Meeting, and other forms of training that have been traditionally done in African American churches. It must be innovative, progressive, relevant, instructive, interesting, and dynamic. Essentially, there are two types of leadership training: pre-service and in-service training.

Pre-Service Leadership Training

Pre-service training is for persons who are either newly elected to a position, been asked to serve in a new position, or who have never held any previous position of leadership in the church. This type of training is usually done for persons who are candidates to be licensed in the ministry, or as a deacon, deaconess, trustee, financial officer, auxiliary president, committee head, etc.

In-Service Training

In-service training is for persons who are currently serving in a leadership position in the church. This type of training is used to help leaders to serve more effectively in their current positions. Training of this type should cover the full gamut of leadership needs within the church.

The world is changing faster than most of us can keep up with. "The constant development of new knowledge and techniques demands that workers in any field continue their learning."[9] The increase in the body of knowledge in all fields makes continuing Christian education mandatory. Without a structured program of instruction, workers will become dry, stagnate, and unable to take advantage of new information, knowledge, skills and techniques.

In-service training in the church should include the whole range of practical skills necessary for effective service and leadership. Further, leadership training must also include biblical and theological training. The Bible is the chief source for all we do and believe. Theological reflection provides the interpretation of those beliefs. Hence, any curriculum design should include biblical and theological training. There is a real need to help those who lead to have a biblically grounded understanding of who we are as believers.

The world in which we live is changing faster than anyone ever imagined. The pace is so rapid that we hardly have time to digest one change before the next generation of technology has burst upon the scene. All of this change has had and will continue to have a definitive impact upon the Christian church. Clearly, we are wiser than the sons of this world. God has called, anointed, and commissioned the church to tear down the kingdom of the enemy. With leaders who are filled with the Holy Spirit, wisdom and the Word of God, we will succeed.

There are a number of voices and new age movements that are competing for the hearts and minds of our people. Gone are the days when people were absolutely loyal to a single church. People are searching for real answers to real problems. They desire and crave real spiritual nurturing and substance. If the African American church is going to play a significant role in the lives of African Americans in the twenty-first century, then we will need to train a whole new generation of leaders for a new generation of Christians.

Dr. Geoffrey V. Guns

Dr. Geoffrey V. Guns is a native of Newport, Rhode Island. He is the son of a Baptist pastor. Dr. Guns is a product of the Norfolk Public School System. He earned his B.S. degree in Business Administration from Norfolk State University in 1972, after which he was commissioned as a U.S. Army Infantry officer. He spent six years in the U.S. Army.

In 1981, he earned his master's of Divinity from the School of Theology, Virginia Union University, graduating Summa Cum Laude. He earned his doctor of Ministry degree from the School of Religion, Howard University in Washington, D.C. in 1985.

Dr. Guns is the pastor of the Second Calvary Baptist Church where he has served for the past 17 years. He is active in his denomination. Dr. Guns serves as the president of the Virginia Baptist State Convention, which has a membership of nearly 700 African American Baptist Churches. He is the immediate past Moderator for the Tidewater-Peninsula Baptist Association. He has served as the Director of the Advanced Leadership Seminar of the National Baptist Congress of Christian Education, National Baptist Convention, U.S.A., Inc.

Dr. Guns serves as the Editor of the Christian Life Study Series, which is being published by the Sunday School Publishing Board of the National Baptist Convention, U.S.A., Inc. Further, he is a member of the Executive Council of the Sunday School Publishing Board, which oversees Christian Education for the National Baptist Convention, U.S.A., Inc. He is the Dean of the Tidewater Church-Wide Institute. He has served as a lecturer and instructor for the B.T.U. and Sunday School Congress of Virginia.

He has written several articles for the Christian Education Informer of the Department of Christian Education of the Sunday School Publishing Board. He is the author of the book, *Church Financial Management:* A Practical Guide For Today's Church Leaders, which is published by Providence House Publishers.

Dr. Guns is a national lecturer and preacher on the subjects of Christian Stewardship and Financial Planning, Money Management for Christian Families, Church Leadership Development, Christian Education and Church Training. He has received numerous awards and recognitions for his community service.

In 1992 and 1998, he led the congregation to complete construction of a $2.5 million dollar church facility. Under his spiritual leadership, Second Calvary has become a leader in social ministry and community outreach. The church is involved in several social ministries that enhance the quality of life of the people in the Broad Creek community. Second Calvary feeds hundreds of families each year, providing spiritual counseling.

The church also sponsors a substance abuse program and alcoholics anonymous group. The church started the Eastside Community Development Corporation, a nonprofit corporation whose mission is to work for social change and economic development in the Eastside of Norfolk, Virginia.

He is married to the former Rosetta Jane Harding of Richmond, Virginia. Rosetta is a licensed social worker and works for the City of Chesapeake Public Schools. They are the parents of two daughters, Kimberly and Nicole.

How to reach Dr. Guns:

Second Calvary Baptist Church

2940 Corprew Avenue

Norfolk, Virginia 23504

1-757-627-8462 office
1-757-464-3442 home

GVGuns@aol.com

For Further Reading

Anderson, Leith. *Dying For Change*. Minneapolis: Bethany House Publishers, 1990.

Bandy, Thomas G. *Moving Off the Map: A Field Guide to Changing the Congregation*. Nashville: Abingdon Press, 1998.

Barna, George. *The Power of Vision*. *Ventura*, CA.: Regal Books, 1992.

Biersdorf, John E. *How Prayer Shapes Ministry*. Bethesda, MD.: Alban Institute, 1992.

Bridges, William. *Managing Transitions: Making the Most of Change*. New York: Addison-Wesley Publishing Co., Inc., 1991.

Briner, Bob and Pritchard, Ray. *The Leadership Lessons of Jesus: A Timeless Model For Today's Leaders*. Nashville: Broadman and Holman, Publishers, 1997.

Brink, Kurt. *Overcoming Pastoral Pitfalls*. St. Louis: Concordia Publishing House, 1997.

Brown, Daniel A. with Larson, Brian. Foreword by Jack Hayford. *The Other Side of Pastoral Ministry: Using Process Leadership To Transform Your Church*. Grand Rapids: Zondervan Publishing Co., 1996.

Carroll, Jackson W. *As One With Authority: Reflective Leadership in Ministry*. Westminster/John Knox Press, 1991.

Conner, Kevin. *The Church in the New Testament*. Portland, OR.: BT Publishing, 1982.

Ezell, Rick. *Ministry On the Cutting Edge: Maintaining Pastoral Effectiveness and Personal Authenticity*. Grand Rapids: Kregel Resources, 1995.

Flynn, Leslie B. *How to Survive in the Ministry*. Grand Rapids: Kregel Publications, 1992.

Gallup, George, Jr. and Lindsay, D. Michael. *Surveying the Religious Landscape: Trends in U.S. Beliefs*. Harrisburg, PA.: Morehouse Publishing, Co., 1999.

Greenleaf, Robert K. *Servant Leadership: A Journey Into the Nature of Legitimate Power and Greatness*. New York: Paulist Press, 1977.

Grenz, Stanley J. and Royd D. Bell. *Betrayal of Trust: Sexual Misconduct in the Pastorate*. Downers Grove, IL.: InterVarsity Press, 1995.

Gushee, David, P. and Jackson, Walter C. *Preparing For Ministry: An Evangelical Approach.* Grand Rapids: Baker Book House, 1998.

Hammett, Edward H. *The Gathered and Scattered Church: Equipping Believers for the 21st Century.* Foreword by Loren Mead. Macon, GA.: Symth & Helwys Publishing, 1999.

Hands, Donald R. and Fehr, Wayne L. *Spiritual Wholeness For Clergy: A New Psychology of Intimacy with God, Self and Others.* Bethesda, MD.: Alban Institute, 1993.

Harrington, Arthur A. *What the Bible Says About Leadership.* Joplin, MO.: College Press Publishing Company, 1985.

Harris, Forrest E., Sr. *Ministry For Social Crisis: Theology and Praxis in the Black Church Tradition.* Macon, GA: Mercer University Press, 1993.

Harris, James H. *Pastoral Leadership: A Black-Church Perspective.* Minneapolis: Fortress Press, 1991.

Hawkins, Thomas R. *The Learning Congregation: A New Vision for Leadership.* Louisville: Westminster John Knox Press, 1997.

Henderson, Perry E. Jr. *The Black Church Credit Union.* Lima, OH.: Fairway Press, 1990.

Herman, Robert D. and Associates. *The Jossey-Bass Handbook of Nonprofit Leadership and Management*. San Francisco: Jossey- Bass Publishers, 1994.

Johnson, Ben Campbell. **Pastoral Spirituality:** *A Focus For Ministry*. Philadelphia: The Westminster Press, 1988.

Johnson, Joseph A., Jr. *Proclamation Theology*. Shreveport, LA.: Fourth Episcopal District Press, 1977.

Kouzes, James M. and Posner Barry Z. Foreword by Tom Peters. *Credibility: How Leaders Gain and Lose It, Why People Demand It*. San Francisco: Jossey-Bass Publishers, 1993.

Lincoln, C. Eric and Mamiya, Lawrence H. *The Black Church in the African American Experience*. Durham, NC: Duke University Press, 1994.

Long, Eddie. *Taking Over: Seizing Your City For God In The New Millennium*. Lake Mary, FL.: Creation House Publishers, 1999.

MacArthur, John F. *The Master's Plan For the Church*. Chicago: Moody Bible Institute, 1991.

Malphurs, Aubrey. Foreword by Haddon W. Robinson. *Developing A Vision for Ministry In the 21st Century*. Grand Rapids: Baker Book House, 1992.

_____. *The Dynamics of Church Leadership*. Edited by Warren W. Wiersbe. Grand Rapids: Baker Book House, 1999.

Marshall, Tom. Foreword by Gerald Coates. *Understanding Leadership*. Ventura, CA.: Renew Books, 1991.

Maxwell, John C. *Developing the Leaders Around You: How To Help Others Reach Their Full Potential*. Nashville: Thomas Nelson Publishers, 1995.

_____. *The 21 Indispensable Qualities Of A Leader: Becoming the Person Others Will Want to Follow*. Nashville: Thomas Nelson Publishers, 1999.

McCalep, George O. Jr. *Faithful Over A Few Things: Seven Critical Church Growth Principles*. Lithonia, GA.: Orman Press, 1996.

_____. *Stir Up the Gifts: Empowering Believers for Victorious Living and Ministry Tasks*. Foreword by Bishop Eddie L. Long. Lithonia, GA.: Orman Press, Inc., 1999.

_____. *Breaking the Huddle*. Foreword by Dr. Jesse Battle, Jr. Lithonia, GA.: Orman Press, Inc., 1997.

McDonough, Reginald M. *Keys to Effective Motivation*. Nashville: Broadman Press, 1979.

Means, James E. Foreword by Bill Hull. *Effective Pastors For A New Century: Helping Leaders Strategize For Success*. Grand Rapids: Baker Book House, 1993.

Murdock, Mike. *The Leadership Secrets of Jesus*. Tulsa, OK.: Honor Books, 1996.

Nouwen, Henri J. M. *Reaching Out: The Three Movements of the Spiritual Life*. New York: Image Books, 1975.

Ogden, Greg. *The New Reformation: Returning the Ministry to the People of God*. Grand Rapids: Zondervan Publishing Co., 1990.

Proctor, Samuel D. and Taylor, Gardner C., with Gary V. Simpson. *We Have This Ministry: The Heart of the Pastor's Vocation*. Valley Forge: Judson Press, 1996.

Ramey, David A. *Empowering Leaders*. Kansas City, MO.: Sheed and Ward, 1991.

Rediger, G. Lloyd. *Clergy Killers: Guidance For Pastors and Congregations Under Attack*. Louisville, KY.: Westminster John Knox Press, 1997.

Reed, Gregory J. *Economic Empowerment Through the Church: A Blueprint for Progressive Community Development*. Foreword by C. Eric Lincoln. Grand Rapids: Zondervan Publishing House, 1994.

Senge, Peter M. *The Fifth Discipline: The Art & Practice of the Learning Organization.* New York: Currency Doubleday, 1990.

Shawchuck, Norman and Heuser, Roger. *Leading the Congregation: Caring For Yourself While Serving The People.* Nashville: Abingdon Press, 1993.

Smith, Bucklin and Associates. *The Complete Guide to Nonprofit Management.* New York: John Wiley & Sons, Inc., 1994.

Smith, Donald P. *Empowering Ministry: Ways to Grow in Effectiveness.* Louisville, KY.: Westminster John Knox Press, 1996.

Smith, J. Alfred, Jr. *Falling In Love With God: Reflections On Prayer.* Bible Study Applications, Colleen Birchett. Chicago: Urban Ministries, Inc., 1997.

Tan, Siang-Yang and Gregg H. Douglas. *Disciplines of the Holy Spirit: How to Connect to the Power and Presence.* Grand Rapids: Zondervan Publishing House, 1997.

Tracy, Diane. *10 Steps To Empowerment: A Common-Sense Guide To Managing People.* New York: Quill William Morrow Company, 1990.

Turner, Nathan, W. *Leading Small Groups: Basic Skills For Church and Community Organizations.* Valley Forge: Judson Press, 1996.

Tyms, James D.. *The Black Church As Nurturing Community, Volume 1.* St. Louis: Hodale Press, 1995.

Weems, Lovett H., Jr. Foreword by Rosabeth Moss Kanter. *Church Leadership: Vision, Team, Culture and Integrity.* Nashville: Abingdon Press, 1993.

Wills, Dick. *Walking to God's Dream: Spiritual Leadership and Church Renewal.* Foreword by James A. Harnish. Nashville: Abingdon Press, 1999.

Wolf, Thomas. *Managing A Nonprofit Organization.* Illustrated by Barbara Carter. New York: Fireside Books, 1984.

End Notes for Introduction

1. Bernard M. Bass, Bass and Stogdill's Handbook of Leadership: Theory, Research, & Managerial Applications, Third Edition, (The Free Press: New York, 1990), p. 3.
2. Ibid., p. 3.
3. Cary Yukl, Leadership in Organizations, Third Edition, (Englewood Cliffs, NJ: Prentice Hall, Inc., 1994), p. 1.
4. Ibid., p. 1.
5. Ralph M. Stogdill, Handbook of Leadership, (New York: The Free Press, 1974) p. 7.
6. Yukl, p. 5.
7. Ibid., pp. 5-6.
8. Bass, p. 6.
9. Ibid., p. 6.
10. George Gallup, Jr. & D. Michael Lindsay, Surveying the Religious Landscape (Harrisburg, PA.: Morehouse Publishing, 1999), pp. 52-55.

End Notes for Chapter One

1. See Gene A.Getz, Sharpening the Focus of the Church. Wheaton, IL.: Victor Books, 1984. Kevin J. Conner, The

Church In the New Testament. Portland, OR.: BT Publishing, 1982. Mal Couch, A Biblical Theology of the Church, Grand Rapids: Kregel Publications, 1999.

2. Kevin J. Conner, The Church in the New Testament, (Portland, OR.: BT Publishing, 1982), p. 15.

3. Joe S. Ellis, The Church On Purpose: Keys to Effective Church Leadership, Foreword by Donald McGavran, (Cincinnati: Standard Publishing Co, 1983), p. 33.

4. G. Willis Bennett, Effective Urban Church Ministry, (Nashville: Broadman Press, 1983), p. 8.

5. Alvin J. Lindgren and Norman Shawchuck, Management for Your Church, (Nashville: Abingdon Press, 1977), p. 23.

6. Bennett, p. 28.

7. The New International Dictionary of New Testament Theology, Vol. 1, s.v. "Church."

8. Ibid.

9. Bennett, p. 28.

10. Ibid.

11. Joe S. Ellis, The Church On Purpose: Keys to Effective Church Leadership, (Cincinnati, Ohio: Standard Publishing Company, 1982), p. 71.

12. NIDNTT, "Fellowship."

13. Ellis, p. 67.

14. Avery T. Willis, Jr., The Biblical Basis of Missions, (Nashville: Convention Press, 1992), p. 13. Edward H. Hammett, The Gathered and Scattered Church:

Equipping Believers for the 21st Century, Foreword by Loren Mead (Macon, GA.: Smyth & Helwys Publishing, Inc., 1999), p. 15.

15. Edward H. Hammett, The Gathered and Scattered Church: Equipping Believers for the 21st Century, (Macon, GA.: Smyth & Helwys Publishing, Inc., 1999) p. 22.

16. Eugene L. Stockwell, Claimed By God for Mission, (New York: World Outlook Press, 1965), p. 138.

17. Lindgren, op. cit., p. 158.

18. Bennett, op. cit. 167.

19. Alvin J. Lindgren and Norman Shawchuck, Management for Your Church, (Nashville: Abingdon Press, 1977), p. 23.

20. Ibid.

21. Michael C. Mack, The Synergy Church: A Strategy for Integrating Small Groups and the Sunday School, (Grand Rapids: Baker Books, 1996), p. 131.

22. Curtis Vaughan, Bible Study Commentary: Ephesians, (Grand Rapids: Zondervan Publishing House, 1977), p. 40.

23. Ibid., p. 41.

24. Ibid.

End Notes for Chapter Two

1. Leonard Goodstein, Timothy Nolan, and J. William Pfeiffer, Applied Strategic Planning: How To Develop A Plan That Really Works, (New York: McGraw-Hill, Inc., 1993), p. 3.

2. Ibid.

3. Robert D. Dale, Leading Edge: Leadership Strategies from the New Testament, (Nashville: Abingdon Press, 1996), p. 3.

4. Aubrey Malphurs, Ministry Nuts and Bolts: What They Don't Teach Pastors in Seminary (Grand Rapids: Kregel Publications, 1997), p. 137.

5. Ibid., p. 138.

6. Ibid., p. 139.

7. Ibid., pp. 141-42.

8. Michael Allison & Jude Kaye, Strategic Planning For Nonprofit Organizations: A Practical Guide and Workbook, (New York: John Wiley & Sons, Inc., 1997), p. 2.

8. Goodstein, Nolan and Pfeiffer, p. 3.

9. Dale, pp. 23-25.

11. Robert K. Greenleaf, Servant Leadership: A Journey Into the Nature of Legitimate Power and Greatness, (New York: Paulist Press, 1977), p. 7.

12. Ibid.

13. Ibid.

14. See Theological Wordbook of the Old Testament, Vol. 2. (Chicago: Moody Press, 1980), p. 825 for a fuller discussion of the word Ahead.

15. Lawrence O. Richards and Clyde Hoeldtke, A Theology of Church Leadership (Grand Rapids: Zondervan Publishing House, 1980), p. 16.

16. Ibid.

17. Ibid.

18. Watchman Nee, Authority and Submission: Living According To The Divine Life In The Body Of Christ (Anaheim, CA.: Living Stream Ministry, 1994), p. 9.

19. Ibid., pp.9-10.

20. Arthur R. Harrington, What The Bible Says About Leadership (Joplin, MO.: College Press Publishing Company), p. 84.

21. Ibid. p. 80.

22. Ibid., pp. 73-77.

23. Ibid., p. 74.

End Notes For Chapter Three

1. J. Oswald Sanders, Spiritual Leadership, Revised Edition (Chicago: Moody Bible Institute, 1980), p. 19.

2. Ibid.

3. Joe S. Ellis, Foreword by Donald McGavran, The Church On Purpose: Keys to Effective Church Leadership (Cincinnati, OH: Standard Publishing Co., 1983) p. 141.

4. Arthur R. Harrington, What The Bible Says About Leadership (Joplin, MO.: College Press Publishing Co., 1985) pp. 78-79.

5. Kenneth O. Gangel, Feeding and Leading: A Practical Handbook on Administration in Churches and Christian Organizations (Grand Rapids: Baker Book House, 1996) p. 31.

End Notes for Chapter Four

1. Joe Ellis, p. 130.
2. Norman Shawchuck and Roger Heuser, Leading the Congregation: Caring for Yourself While Serving the People (Nashville: Abingdon Press, 1993), p. 119.
3. Ibid., p. 121.
4. Ibid.
5. Ibid.
6. Ibid., pp. 121-22.
7. Quoted by Kevin J. Conner, The Church In The New Testament (Portland, OR.: BT Publishing, 1982), p. 218.

End Notes for Chapter Five

1. Norman Shawchuck and Roger Heuser, Leading the Congregation, (Nashville: Abingdon Press, 1993), p. 167.
2. "Next Population Bulge Shows Its Might," Wall Street Journal, Feb. 3, 1997, B, p.1.
3. Quoted in the Foreword of, Eddie Long, Taking Over: Seizing Your City For God In The New Millennium (Lake Mary, FL.: Creation House, 1999), p. iiv.
4. Shawchuck and Heuser, Leading the Congregation, p. 15.
5. Simon Chan, Spiritual Theology: A Systematic Study Of The Christian Life (Downers Grove, IL.: InterVarsity Press, 1998), p. 150.
6. Shawchuck and Heuser, p. 37.
7. Jackson Carroll, As One With Authority: Reflective Leadership In Ministry, (Louisville: Westminster/John Knox Press, 1991), p. 36.

8. Ibid., pp. 36-37.

9. Eddie Long, p. 15.

10. Theological Dictionary Of The New Testament, "Exousia," Edited by Geoffrey W. Bromiley, Abridged in One Volume (Grands Rapids: William B. Eerdams Publishing Co., pp. 238-40.

End Notes for Chapter Six

1. Throughout the discussion on the role of deacons I am also referring to the deaconesses as well. I recognize that all congregations do not consider deacons and deaconesses to be on the same spiritual level. There are some churches that have ordained women to be deacons. I believe that deacon and deaconess refers to the same function within the church. Therefore, a deaconess is equivalent to a deacon in function and stature.

2. Alexander Strauch, The New Testament Deacon: Minister of Mercy (Littleton, CO: Lewis and Roth Publishers, 1992) p. 16.

3. Ibid.

4. Ibid., p. 33.

5. Ibid., p. 34.

6. Arthur R. Harrington, Leadership, pp. 207-36. This is the best and most comprehensive discussion that I have seen on the issue and question of boards in the church. I strongly recommend Harrington's work as a source of insight and information on this subject.

7. Ibid, pp. 211-12.

8. James A. Sheffield, Church Officer and Committee Guidebook, (Nashville: Convention Press, 1976), p. 29.

End Notes for Chapter Seven

1. Joel Arthur Barker, Paradigms: The Business of Discovering the Future (New York: HarperBusiness, 1992) p. 32.
2. Burt Nanus, Leading the Way to Organizational Renewal, (Portland, OR.: Productivity Press, Inc., 1996), p. 3.
3. Barker, p. 204.
4. Ibid.
5. C. Eric Lincoln and Lawrence H. Mamiya, The Black Church in the African American Experience, Seventh Printing (Durham, NC: Duke University Press, 1994) pp. 322-24.
6. Ibid.
7. Bobby William Austin, Editor, Repairing The Breach: National Task Force on African-American Men and Boys, (Dillon, CO.: Alpine Guild, Inc., 1996), p. 23.

End Notes for Chapter Eight

1. McCalep, Faithful Over A Few Things, p. 47.
2. Shawchuck & Heuser, Leading, p. 165.
3. Ibid., p. 166.
4. Aubrey Malphurs, Doing Church: A Biblical Guide for Leading Ministries Through Change (Grand Rapids: Kregel Publications, 1999) p. 15.
5. Jim Petersen, Church Without Walls: Moving Beyond Traditional Barriers (Colorado Springs, CO.: NAVPRESS, 1992) p. 146.

6. Ibid., p. 167.

7. William Bridges, Managing Transitions: Making the Most of Change (New York: Addison-Wesley Publishing Co., Inc., 1991) p. 3.

8. Ibid.

9. Ibid.

End Notes for Chapter Nine

1. Burt Nanus, Visionary Leadership, Foreword by Warren Bennis (San Francisco: Jossey-Bass Publishers, 1992), p. 8.

2. R. Robert Cueni, The Vital Church Leader, Edited by Herb Miller (Nashville: Abingdon Press, 1991), p. 36.

3. Aubrey Malphurs, Developing A Vision For Ministry In The 21st Century, Second Edition, Foreword by Haddon W. Robinson (Grand Rapids: Baker Books, 1999), p. 32.

4. Robert K. Greenleaf, Servant Leadership: A Journey Into the Nature of Legitimate Power and Greatness (New York: Paulist Press, 1977) p. 16.

5. George Barna, The Power of Vision (Ventura, CA.: Regal Books, 1992), p. 28.

6. Ibid., pp. 29-31.

End Notes for Chapter Ten

1. Reginald M. McDonough, Keys to Effective Motivation (Nashville: Broadman Press, 1979), p. 79.

2. William H. Cook, Success, Motivation, and the Scriptures, Foreword by Bill Bright/Introduction by Jack R. Taylor (Nashville: Convention Press, 1974), pp. 99-100.

3. Reginald M. McDonough, Working With Volunteer Leaders In The Church, (Nashville: Broadman Press, 1976) pp. 50-65.

4. Ibid., p. 51.

5. Ibid.

6. Ibid., p. 77.

7. Dayle M. Smith, Ph.D., The Eleven Keys To Leadership (Chicago: IL.: Contemporary Books, 1997) pp. 105-06.

8. Peter M. Senge, The Fifth Discipline: The Art & Practice of the Learning Organization, (New York: Currency Doubleday, 1990), p. 4.

End Notes for Chapter Eleven

1. McDonough, Working With Volunteer Leaders, p. 37. I suggest that you take a look at Nathan W. Turner's work, Leading Small Groups: Basic Skills For Church And Community Organizations. Valley Forge: Judson Press, 1996. In this book he offers several small group leadership skill workshops.

2. John Maxwell, Developing The Leaders Around You: How To Help Others Reach Their Full Potential (Nashville: Thomas Nelson Publishers, 1995), p. 3.

3. Thomas R. Hawkins, The Learning Congregation: A New Vision of Leadership (Louisville: Westminster John Knox Press, 1997), p. 26.

4. Gareth Walden Icenogle, Biblical Foundations for Small Group Ministry, (Downers Grove, IL.: InterVarsity Press, 1994), p. 161.

5. Peter M. Senge, p. 139.

6. George O. McCalep, Jr., Stir Up The Gifts: Empowering Believers for Victorious Living and Ministry Tasks, Foreword by Bishop Eddie L. Long (Lithonia, GA.: Orman Press, Inc., 1999), p. 17.

7. Lyle E. Schaller, Strategies for Change, (Nashville: Abingdon Press, 1993), p. 10.

8. C. Doug Bryan, Learning to Teach, Teaching to Learn: A Holistic Approach, (Nashville: Broadman and Holman Publishers, 1993), p. 146.

9. Mary Alice Douty Edwards, Leadership Development and the Worker's Conference, (Nashville: Abingdon, 1967), p. 68.